"Lest We Forget

The Story of Normacot

Written and Researched

by

Mary Wilkinson Freeman

THREE COUNTIES PUBLISHING LIMITED

Published by

THREE COUNTIES PUBLISHING LIMITED

P.O. Box 435
Leek, Staffordshire
ST13 5TB
01538 380910

ISBN 0 9535239 0 X

Typeset in Aster New Opti 11pt by PhotoPrint of Leek
and Printed in England by Cheshire County Press Limited

"LEST WE FORGET"

DEDICATION

To

My Mother, Florence May
Wilkinson
1904 - 1978
who made all things possible.

My Brother, Robert William
Wilkinson L.L.B.,Hons. (London)
1938 - 1981
for his love and friendship.

The origin of the 'Eternal Knot' design can be traced to 5,000 B.C. It depicts an unbroken path without beginning or end and is a perfect expression of the boundlessness of God and the infinite diversity of His Creation.

CONTENTS

THE AUTHOR

Mary Freeman was born in Torquay and came to Normacot in 1934. She attended the Church of England Infant and Junior Schools before winning a scholarship to Thistley Hough Grammar School for Girls (1940 - 1947).

After Higher School Certificate she studied at the Royal Manchester College of Music taking Diplomas in Teaching and Performing (1947 − 51). As a Mezzo-soprano, Mary specialised in recital work throughout the Midlands during the 1950's and early 1960's. Locally she appeared as soloist with the Newcastle String Orchestra, the Daleian Singers and at the Kathleen Ferrier Hall with Harry Vincent, founder of the Etruscan Choir. It was at this time she broadcast from Birmingham and also on B.B.C. Radio Stoke, before establishing the 'Arts at One' lunch-time recitals at the City Museum, prior to the building of the new Recital Theatre.

As a member of the third generation of a teaching family, Mary taught music in City and County Secondary Schools before becoming Head of Music and Principal Lecturer at Cauldon College (1963 - 1981)   Her service to the community has included sixteen years as a Justice of the Peace for the City of Stoke on Trent and nine years as a Governor of Blythe Bridge High School.

A keen golfer since retirement, Mary became Lady Captain of Leek (Birchall) Golf Club in 1994 and was elected to the Board of Management, as a Director in 1997, with responsibility as Chairman of Health and Safety.

Her ties with Normacot have remained strong with 'family memory' spanning almost one hundred years, so Mary decided to write about people who had influenced the development of Normacot and it's quality of life during that period of time.

K. Edwards

ACKNOWLEDGEMENTS.

To my husband, Grenville Freeman, for his hours of dedicated proof reading, patience and love.

Sue Corns for transferring my often untidy manuscripts onto disc, willingly and efficiently.

Father Samuel Carter for data relating to the Church of the Holy Evangelists.

Mr. M. Akram of the Longton Mosque for his help and hospitality.

Mrs. Nora Lovatt for permission to reproduce photographs from the Lovatt Collection.

Kenneth Edwards for his skilled treatment of old photographs and his unique pictures of the Church of the Holy Evangelists, Normacot and Longton Mosque.

Keith Warburton for his research on maps relating to Normacot.

The City Archivist, Mr. Peter Foden and his staff who have assisted me at all times.

The people of Normacot who have shared their memories and time whenever it was necessary. Without their help and friendship it would have been impossible to write this book.

"What is the use of a book," thought Alice, *"without pictures and conversations?,"*

(Lewis Carroll).

NORMACOT CIRCA 1930.

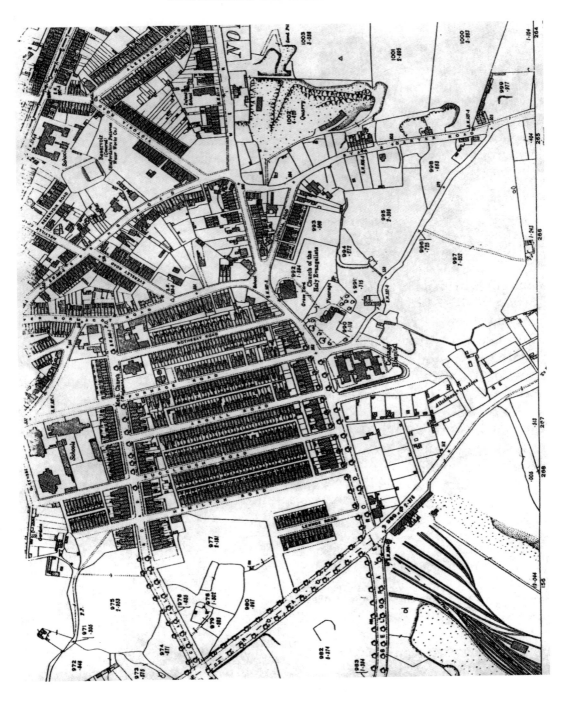

Preface

The Parish of Normacot has provided skilled workers for the pottery industry for well over one hundred and fifty years, yet it has never possessed a bottle oven of its own!

As a child in the 1930's, I realised that the village inherited a fair percentage of the smoke which hung over Longton like a pall. On the traditional washday Monday, with all the difficulties of boiling water in the copper, and hard work at the 'dolly-tub', matters always reached a climax when the sheets were hung outside to dry. Unless this was fitted into the schedule of factory 'firing time', soot seemed to descend onto each item of washing from every point of the compass!

Today, Normacot can look back on an ancient and interesting history. Through the centuries, its boundaries have been defined by tracks, then toll roads and now, by the new A50 which follows the old Roman road which ran from Uttoxeter to Chesterton.

Artefacts of the Neolithic period have been found which provide evidence of a settlement some 4,000 years ago, while a 'collared' urn, circa 1,000 BC was discovered near to natural springs in the area of Ludwall Road.

The Roman period of occupation gave rise to numerous archeological finds; tools, coins of regular and irregular shapes and a pair of silver bracelets which were found in a Lightwood Road garden.

The place name, 'Normacot, Normanescote, Normacott,' probably originated when a man from further north decided to settle in the area and built or occupied a dwelling. 'Cottar,' is a Scottish name for a peasant occupying a, 'cott', for which he has to give his labour. On early maps the village is called, 'Furnace,' denoting the smelting works situated behind the present church-yard, in the days of the Foley family.

Our conquerors, the Normans, kept meticulous accounts! In the Domesday Book, 'Normanescote' was a Hide (120 acres) and held by Richard the Forester. "There is land for one plough, (a team of 8 oxen). The wood is three furlongs in length and two furlongs wide". The population at this time was probably no more than ten or twelve people.

Over the next two centuries there was, inevitably, much inter-marriage between Norman and Saxon. The names of noblewomen revealed in the chronicles of the time, evoke the atmosphere of a colourful and exciting period in history. Petronilla de Bidulf, Aline of Darlaston, Hawisia de Verdun, her daughter, Dionysia, who retained her maiden name after marriage!

By 1215, Henry II's 'New Forest' preservation order was removed by King John, so farms and heathlands were able to develop. This affected Normacot because Henry de Audley acquired the village from the King and in 1223 wrote, "I give and concede to my monks (Hulton Abbey) all my lands."

The Cistercians developed the land quickly, Normacot Grange, (previously Meir Aerodrome, now Meir Park) remained common land, while the nearby hills were given over to sheep. Wool was a valuable asset and for that reason the monks extended grazing areas as far away as Blurton.

Henry VIII, responsible for the dissolution of the monasteries, granted lands belonging to Trentham Priory at Cocknage and Lightwood to the Duke of Suffolk, who in due course sold them to James Leveson, an ancestor of the Sutherland family. Due to this transaction, the close and caring association of the Dukes of Sutherland with Normacot, had it roots as early as the mid 1500's.

By the mid 1600's, Normacot's population had increased to approximately 50 people. The village was on it's way, developing it's own character and skills within the framework of a fast changing outside world and its 'entrepreneurs.'

During the 1700's, Normacot experienced the results of industry at Furnace Mill, the ravages to the terrain left behind by the iron-masters and an immense increase in travel along the new Turnpike Road (A50) and the 13th century Stone Road.

The quick growth of the pottery industry brought an ever growing population to Longton, with a rapid overspill of houses and factories to nearby areas. All public amenities were woefully inadequate, lagging behind the dire need of the people. The 'pursuit of happiness' did not stand a chance in the face of profit versus survival.

Normacot escaped much of this onslaught, probably due to its position between roads which took people to more important places; those which dealt directly with commerce and industry. There was no real need to come to Normacot unless one lived there. The only apparent blot on the village's 'escutcheon' was the Furnace Inn, a place of exceedingly low life, with predictable and allied activities!

The Dukes of Sutherland feature strongly in the history and development of Normacot during the 1800's. The first Duke, George Granville Leveson Gower (1758-1833) known as the 'Leviathan of Wealth' was fortunate in having James

Lock as his agent. With his help and advice great improvements were made to all the Sutherland estates.

George Granville Leveson Gower the second Duke (1786-1861) endeavoured to make his estate, as perfect as possible, again with the help of Lock and his son George. By the 1850's a general 'social conscience' was on the horizon of many employers and at last some consideration was given for the housing of their workers and tenants.

The Duke, a pioneer in these matters, set his standards high. In the late 1850's and early 1860's, Dresden was created on a, 'grid-iron' pattern; and it is obvious that there was nothing haphazard in his planning. When it was Normacot's turn for development, the third Duke, George Granville Leveson Gower (1828-1892) required the standards to be even higher than those in Dresden.

The plan for his 'Garden Village' was once again based on the 'grid-iron' system; each house had a living room, scullery and two bedrooms. The main rooms were 12 feet square and nine feet high, with the outside wall measuring nine inches. By building over the entry space, every second terraced house had a third bedroom.

Each street was a minimum of 36 feet wide and every house had a yard with an outhouse, a 'privvie' and space for a vegetable garden. This ensured independence for the family in times of unemployment. It is significant to note that by 1884, the Duke's own requirements for housing, were incorporated into the by-laws for the Borough.

The third Duke was a wise and generous man. Rents for his houses were modest, but tenants were expected to behave and his agents kept registers on a scale ranging from 'Industrious', to 'Bad'. Arrears, drunkenness, idleness or living with another man's wife resulted in loss of tenancy. However, extra care and attention was always given to the aged and infirm.

These moral disciplines were accepted because unless luck prevailed, the workhouse was the only alternative!

During this period in Normacot's history, the third Duke's sense of commitment to the people of his estate, his sense of duty and his considered view of both the present and possibilities for the future, was inspired.

He re-opened Florence Colliery, naming it after his sister, Lady Florence Chaplin. He gave the land on which Longton Cottage Hospital stands as well as the forty five acres for a public park to commemorate 'Fifty Glorious Years' of Queen Victoria's reign. He gave the land for the building of the Sutherland

Institute and through his close friendship with the Prince of Wales, made it possible for the people of Longton and Normacot, to actually see their future King, when he came to lay the foundation stone.

Anyone visiting Normacot today can still see the geometrical lines of well preserved terraced houses in roads which bear the proud names of Sutherland possessions, each with its own place in history; Rothesay, Argyll, Buccleuch, Hamilton and Lennox. Chaplin Road, was the main thoroughfare in the village 'grid' system and contained bay windowed type houses as well as the usual terraced houses.

Normacot is now the home for people of different races and religions; generally life is peaceful and prosperous for most of its inhabitants. Again the village is developing new skills and a new character in the framework achieved for it by the Dukes of Sutherland.

Unless you live in Normacot, there is still no real reason to visit. The old road to the Meir is now a secondary road with no direct access to the A50 and is relatively quiet for the latter part of the 20th century.

The hasty traveller still passes by on the A50 and the outside world appears to have better things to do than make the necessary detour to what seems to be a fortified settlement behind the retaining walls of the new motorway.

However, much is happening in Normacot now and much more has happened in the past.

So, **'Lest we Forget'**, we must proceed!

FURNACE MILL AND FARM

Watery Lane is a peaceful place, even in the twentieth century. Thirty years ago, it was wide enough for a horse drawn cart to travel comfortably from Belgrave Road to Star and Garter Road, and then on to the outlying farms of Lightwood. Today, it is no more than an overgrown footpath, shielded from the noise of traffic, by high hedgerows where wild flowers and berries still grow in profusion, well guarded by the expanse of what used to be called, 'Lester's Fields.'

This must have been the scene when the first, industry came to Normacot in 1580, namely an iron works on the site of what came to be known as, 'Furnace Mill.' Leased by the Leveson's of Trentham Hall, to John Oldcoatt of Talke, this was to be the beginning of the mill's long history. There was a plentiful supply of charcoal and limestone, while water power was available nearby. 1610 saw the furnace worked by Thomas Hunt when changes and developments were taking place rapidly.

A new smelting furnace was established by 1620 and was situated behind the present churchyard. This was also the year in which the Furnace Inn was built; in the late nineteenth century it became Normacot Vicarage. On early maps, the whole area is referred to as 'Furnace' and not Normacot. The Inn catered for the local people and also the, 'new breed' of business men; the iron masters, their employees and the growing number of travellers using the old Roman road, (A50) half a mile away or using the thirteenth century road from Longton to Stone (Lightwood Road).

Its status of being a Coaching Inn, did little to improve the behaviour of those who stayed or visited. Notorious for cock-fighting, dog fighting and bear baiting, drunkenness and low life generally, it comes as no surprise to learn that the village stocks were just outside the Inn, with mine host as keeper of the keys!

The Birmingham ironmasters, the Foleys, bought Longton Manor circa 1651. They already owned property in Oakamoor and with their business empire spreading to Tintern, in the Wye Valley, one can only try to realise the impact they must have had on, 'Furnace.' The first industrial landscape was created in Normacot at this time and the Foley's continued to increase their production of pig-iron with the inevitable environmental results.

With the constant need for charcoal, parts of the ancient Lightwood Forest disappeared; pig-iron pits were everywhere and the waste disposed of with

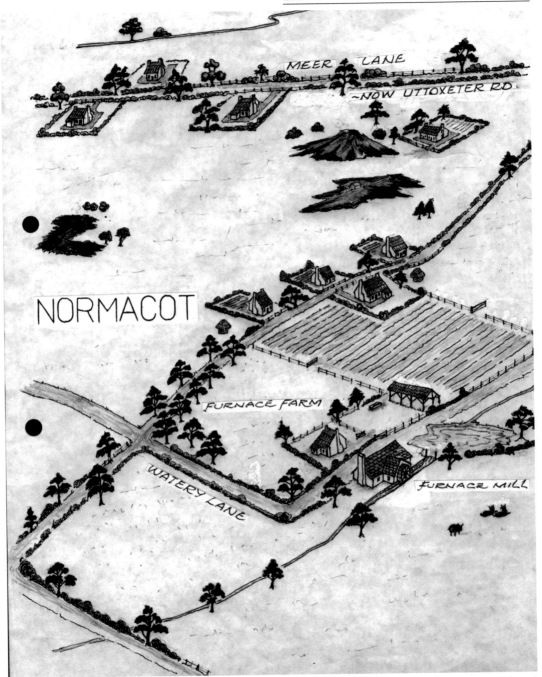

J. Cook (Hanley Reference Library)

Map of Furnace Mill and Farm circa 1700

scant regard for the future. The raised ground on which the nearby Cottage Hospital was built in 1890, bore much evidence of industrial debris from this period. Matters became so bad, that in 1679, the Newcastle Court ordered the Foley's to, "Fill in all dangerous pits." Now, day in and day out, the idyllic quiet of Normacot was disturbed by the noise of forge hammers and power bellows. The spring from Leod's (or Ludd's) well, in Ludwall Road, joined the, 'race' of Furnace Brook which gushed from under the sandhills of Star and Garter Road and Meir Heath, thus providing the necessary power to drive these implements.

Energy for smelting came from the water wheel which operated the bellows system. The Ludwall Spring, was then dammed to create a large pool, enabling the Foley's to greatly increase their out-put of pig-iron, over a twenty year period. In spite of this activity, there were few inhabitants and even by 1666 Normacot was still an undeveloped rural area. 1702 saw Furnace Mill leased by the first of the Lane family, followed by the elder Reverend Obadiah Lane in 1749. A new lease was obtained in 1758 by the younger Reverend Obadiah Lane, who continued business interests with the Foleys until 1773. Smelting finished on the site circa 1750.

The coming of Turnpike roads in the mid 1700's began the real development of Longton as a significant centre and also made Normacot more accessible; the Turnpike road to Meir opened in 1759 and the one to Trentham in 1777. By now, the growing pottery industry changed the work of Furnace Mill from grinding flint into serving the needs of the, 'potters,' when it was owned by the influential and wealthy Heathcote family in 1778. As needs continued to change, so did the work of the Mill when Thomas Gibbs, of Lane End, and his partners John and Thomas Cooper, of Cheadle, decided that for a short time it would exist as a cotton mill.

By the 1851 census, this work had disappeared, and the Mill, ever resilient, served as a cornmill and farm during the lease of George Plant, of Eccleshall and later that of Alfred Glover, of Gom's Mill, who as a flint grinder leased a cottage and a field. Leases in 1882 and 1899 were taken out by the Bakewell family and E. J. Froggatt Esq., respectively, for the same purpose. The family of William Lester were the first tenants of the twentieth century, leasing the property from the Duke of Sutherland for farming and dairy purposes.

The Lesters were held in high regard in Normacot and were closely involved with the life of both the church and the school. Wm Lester was Church Warden from 1905 - 1909, sharing these duties for the first three years with Mr. Wm Wilkinson, Headmaster, and the last year with Mr. T. C. Wild, pottery manufacturer, the founder of the St. Mary's works in Uttoxeter Road.

Wm Lester at Harvest Time

Lovatt

In 1919, the Duke's Trentham Estate was for sale, and so, of course, was 'Furnace Mill Farm'. It was bought by British Glue and Chemicals Limited, who supplied calcined bone to local china factories. Interestingly, water power was used on the site until the early 1940's.

Today, Lester's Farm comprises two properties; Mill House West, the home of Mr. and Mrs. L. Leighton, and Mill House East, the adjoining property of Mr. and Mrs. Barry Harrington. This is the farm which I remembered from my childhood. The front door in the picture (page 16) is now to the right, while today, the old stables on the left, serve as a large modern garage.

The old farmyard has become a paved courtyard, and the visitor enters through an ornamental gate set in high walls. These shield the large informal gardens, shaded

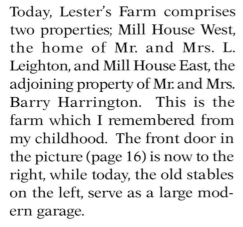

Furnace Mill Farm, Normacot.

LOT 412.

Very desirable

SMALL FARM

especially suitable for occupation in conjunction with a milk seller and dairyman's business, situate in the heart of island area bounded by the Belgrave, Ludwall, Star and Garter and Stone Roads, and intersected by Watery Lane.

The Premises consist of

Roomy and substantially built Dwelling House, together with Out-Offices, Farm Buildings and 16 Acres or thereabouts of rich Old Turf.

THE HOUSE contains Two Sitting Rooms, Kitchen, Scullery, Pantry, Landing, Five Bedrooms. Wash House and Coal House with Lofting over, E.C.

THE FARM BUILDINGS consist of Cow House with tying for four, do. with tying for three, both with Lofting over, Calf Kit, Meal House and Poultry House. Good Garden.

The Potteries Water is laid on to the Premises.

THE LAND—as has already been mentioned—is entirely under permanent pasture, has been exceptionally well farmed, and is at present in very productive condition.

It possesses the additional advantage of a good natural water supply.

Tenant :—Mr. WILLIAM LESTER.

141

by ancient trees and newer flowering shrubs from the outside world. As I walked to the front door one summer evening, I felt that the twentieth century could have been a figment of my imagination. There was no traffic noise and I could hear quite clearly the sound of a light breeze high in the trees and very faintly, the sound of water flowing gently and steadily at the top of the garden.

*Lester's Farm
circa 1910*

Lovatt

Later, after coffee and conversation, Barry and I walked the length and breadth of the property. As we looked back at Mill House, he told me that the roof and its timbers had been replaced, as had all the windows and doors. Most of the work he had achieved himself and so was able to make sure that the renovations were in keeping with the character of the original house. During this time, many different types of tile and brick had been discovered. Malting tiles with their smoked undersides, tapered tiles with a hole, these latter probably having been made by George Edwards of Cheddleton. Some building bricks were of the, 'Biscuit' type with rubble inside their casing. Barry told me that Chadwick's, the pottery manufacturers, were often able to make a good profit from rubble in the local mines by manufacturing this type of brick. Others to be found in the house and its outbuildings were Flemish Bond and English Bond; these were used as 'headers' and, 'stretchers' to form a patterned construction.

Where the Lesters had their boar sty is now a large grassed area which leads to Furnace Brook at the top of the garden. This is what I had come to see! The brook still comes, as it has for centuries, from behind the Church and under the grave yard. It then cascades some five feet into a crystal clear pool. The grey, brown and white pebbles at the bottom of the pool are worn smooth and round by the gushing and flowing of the spring on its way to the playing fields of Watery Lane, and beyond. Cautiously, I expressed some doubt about the purity of the water for drinking purposes, but Barry assured me that rigorous chemical tests had shown it to be pure and safe and it did not need to be boiled!

Barry, who is an engineer, had also ascertained the energy 'output' of the brook. "It produces one gallon of water every ten seconds which results in a steady 600 watts of energy. Perhaps when I have time, I can harness the brook and have enough energy to run a deep freeze and a refrigerator" said Barry, as we made our way back to Mill House. When I left the quietness and tranquillity of the garden, I knew that Mill House East and its long history, was in safe hands. It is unlikely that forge hammers and power bellows will disturb Watery Lane ever again and the only evidence of an industrial past is retained nearby in the name of 'Furnace Road.' I had enjoyed an evening of idyllic quiet such as it might have been in 1580, but in the comfortable and secure knowledge that now it was with, 'All mod cons.'

Lovatt

'The Long Way Home'
Watery Lane circa 1910
Note the wooden edged slates and knickerbockers.

THE DUKE'S CHURCH

THE CHURCH OF THE HOLY EVANGELISTS

Normacot Church Choir 1902

Church Archive

Back Row L - R
Mr. Bridgwood, Mr. G. Dale,
Mr. Stonier
? Mr. W. Rowley

Front Row L - R
Mr. O. Johnson, Rev. Wm. Barnes
Hunter (Curate at Edensor, Assistant
Curate at Normacot.), Mr. Wm. Kirk

'All is safely gathered in'.
The decorated font circa 1905
presented by Charles Harvey of Meir
House in 1847

Lovatt

THE CHURCH OF THE HOLY EVANGELISTS NORMACOT

The Early Days

There were no women priests or flying bishops and no discussions on the possibility of one sex marriages when Normacot's existence as a separate parish, with it's own church and resident incumbent was made possible by Canon John Hutchinson, M.A., and George Granville, the second Duke of Sutherland!

John Hutchinson (1793 -1865) was priest in charge of Blurton from 1818 and Vicar of Blurton from 1834 - 65. His responsibilities included, 'Meir Church' from 1835 - 47. In reality, this was the National School which stood opposite the site of the present church. Built in 1833, it was licensed for services from 1835. This building was the basis of the future Church of England Junior School.

Hutchinson's dedication to all his parishioners, linked with his vision of a church for the growing population of the, 'Normanescote' of the Domesday Book, would have been useless, without the generosity and forward planning of the Duke.

A Vestry Meeting at Blurton on the 13th February 1845, chaired by Hutchinson, decided that the following important matters should be established. Normacot, for ecclesiastical purposes, was to be part of Blurton, not Trentham, and the Duke of Sutherland would build a new church with a burial ground nearby.

Only the best was good enough for the people of Normacot! The architect was the young and talented Gilbert Scott, destined for a knighthood and national fame in later years. The design chosen by the Duke was that of a village church; even today, with the bell tower removed because of subsidence in 1951, the graceful style of its true English architecture is retained.

The church stands at the junction of Normacot and Meir Roads and was completed in two years. With the purchase of Furnace Inn and its refurbishment as a Vicarage, the total cost came to £2,200, Scott's fee being £160. It is interesting to note that draining the entire site, with its many natural springs came to £33.10.10; the levelling of land and making paths in the churchyard cost £18.4.0. Expenditure at the Parsonage for a driveway was £7.0.0 while the building of an extensive stone boundary wall, which can still be seen today, cost the princely sum of £2.10.6. The builder of the church, William Evans of Ellastone, was well known for work of high quality and had the added distinction of being the uncle of George Elliot, the novelist. His fee was £1,766.

Unlike the town churches of the day, Normacot had no gallery. The side aisles are connected to both nave and chancel, and inspite of seating for four hundred people, one hundred of which were paid for by wealthy parishioners, one's gaze has always been drawn directly and easily, to the altar. Six circular red sandstone pillars arch upwards to the rafters of the nave, enhancing the feeling of space and light which pervades every part of the church. Prior to the building and consecration of the present church, gifts to the 'School which was a Church' included a Lectern Bible from the Duke and a chalice and Patten given by Ralph Bourne, Lord of the Manor of Hilderstone. On the 23rd July 1847, the great day of Consecration arrived, and the, 'Staffordshire Courier' gave the following detailed report.

CONSECRATION OF NORMACOT CHURCH.

Soon after eleven o'clock on Friday week the Lord Bishop of the diocese, attended by the Archdeacon of Stafford, was received on the ground by a numerous body of the clergy, not only of the neighbourhood, but from various places more or less distant; among whom we noticed the Revds. Messrs. Edwards, Hutchinson, and Oliver; Aitkens, rural dean of Stoke; Professor Blunt, of Cambridge; Lloyd, D. N. Walton, Dr. Stock, Lucas and Kitchen, of Stone; R. Bourne Baker, rural dean of Stone; Boucher, of Dilhorne; Armstrong, Tooth, Plant, Tyson, Wright, Grant, Grey, Minton, Ewens, Clark, Porter, Shooter, Allen, Greenwood, Wood, Sneyd, Twemlow, &c., in all about 45. His lordship, followed by the clergy, proceeded to the west door of the church, and there receiving the petition to consecrate, the impressive service was forthwith begun, the church having, previous to his lordship's arrival, completely filled with a congregation collected chiefly from the immediate neighbourhood. The prayers were read by the Rev. John Hutchinson, perpetual curate of Blurton; the lessons by the Rev. W. H. Oliver, the incumbent of Normacot church; the epistle by the Rev. E. J. Edwards, rural dean of Trentham; the gospel by the Ven. the Archdeacon of Stafford. Then followed the "Old 100th Psalm," usually sung on these occasions we believe,—and sung on this occasion, as it very seldom is,—to the tune called Savoy, as Luther really composed that noble melody. We may say of the singing here, altogether, that it was good—that is, pure, plain, in good tune, and correct time, and therefore the whole congregation could and did join in it. The sermon was preached by the Lord Bishop, and was an earnest, hearty, and affecting exhortation to his hearers, founded on Isaiah, chap. 5, v. 1—8. It was wholly taken up in explaining and enforcing those most solemn words, nor did his lordship make from the pulpit any other than a passing allusion to the charitable act of the Duke of Sutherland, the giver of this church and parsonage for the use chiefly of the poor on this part of his Grace's estates. During the offertory, read by the Archdeacon, a collection was made towards certain incidental expenses connected, we believe, with the consecration, which amounted to £61 10s., including £5 from J. L. Ricardo, Esq., M.P., and £5 from R. E. Heathcote, Esq. The bishop was pleased to remit the usual consecration fee.

The consecration of the church was immediately followed by that of the burial ground, after which a numerous party, both of laity and clergy, repaired to the school-room, where they found awaiting a collation, one glance at which bespoke it—by the exquisite beauty and size of the fruits, especially the pine apples—to have been furnished by the same princely bounty which had provided the far more enduring gift which had formed the foundation for this most interesting day's proceedings. His lordship took an early opportunity, during the repast, to propose, in terms of the most graceful and happy allusion, the toast of "health and happiness to the Duke and Duchess of Sutherland;" soon after which his lordship withdrew, amid the cheers and good wishes of all assembled.

This church, which is dedicated by the name of the Holy Evangelists, contains about three hundred free, and one hundred appropriated sittings, on open benches, duly provided with kneelers, and is, we understand, the fifth or sixth church which the Duke of Sutherland has erected within the last few years at his sole cost. In the present case very handsome offerings have been made to the church by individuals desirous of testifying their sense of the importance to the neighbourhood of this recent provision for its spiritual wants. Chas. Harvey, Esq., of the Mear House, and the different members of his family have presented besides the font, six stained windows for the chancel, executed by the able hand of Mr. Wailes; and Herbert Minton, Esq., has given the encaustic tiles with which the chancel is laid, and also two, of a large size, for the nave, one of which exhibits the shield of the founder, and the other that of the bishop of the diocese. The style of architecture is early English advancing into decorated. A side aisle, in lieu of a gallery, is attached both to the nave and chancel; and the church is thus enriched with 6 arches which, in addition to a chancel, and of unusual breadth and airiness, give great character to the interior. Mr. Scott is the architect, and the fullest justice has been done to his designs by Mr. W. Evans, of Ellastone, the builder. To the gift of a church the Duke of Sutherland has added that of a parsonage, having converted a public house on the spot into a most commodious private dwelling. The population for whose benefit the church is intended is about 1,100 in number, and the church will be opened for stated service (see advertisement) to-morrow, when collections will be made in support of the day and Sunday schools, in which about one-eighth of the population are instructed.

The dignitaries, both temporal and spiritual then departed, as did the politicians, reporters and the Duke himself; the time for hard work had arrived! The last six lines of the report put this work into true perspective; namely the establishing of the new church, it's Sunday School, and a Day School was about to begin. The young Reverend W. H. Oliver M.A., had been priest in charge for two years from 1846 and was then replaced by the Reverend William

Hombersley M.A., who was resident priest from 1849 until 1853, when he became the first Vicar of Normacot until his resignation in 1875.

Hombersley worked hard in all the areas required by his parishioners; equal regard was given to their everyday needs as well as to their spiritual welfare. By his steady and thorough groundwork in this new situation, he made possible the outstanding work achieved by his successor, Reverend John Hutchinson M.A., who served the Church of the Holy Evangelists from 1875 until his death in 1892. County records show that in the year of his appointment, Queen Anne's Bounty of £400 was received in the form of an endowment to the Church.

The second Vicar of Normacot, J. R. Hutchinson M.A., was the son of the man who had helped to make possible Normacot's separate existence as a parish, namely, the Reverend John Hutchinson, of Blurton. Ecclesiastical and social circles must have been close-knit during these early days in Normacot, so it is not surprising to find that J. R. Hutchinson, married Ruth, the daughter of his predecessor, Reverend Wm. Hombersley. This sketch of the original Normacot Church underlines this fact; it is by Mrs. A. B. Bailey of Shooters Hills, Lightwood, who was the sister of Reverend John Hutchinson.

Normacot Church - Original Sketch

With the appointment of JRH, at the age of twenty-seven, we see a period of significant growth and change in the parish. Luckily, the church had chosen a priest whose energy and strength of purpose could cope with the problems of poverty, drunkenness, poor conditions at home and at work, as well as the ever present fear of ill-health and epidemics. JRH formed a Church of England Temperance Society; a formidable task when so many private houses in Normacot retailed beer.

A savings scheme was started to ensure that families were able to live in some sort of financial stability, however, minimal. Drunkenness and poverty went hand in hand, as is shown in this Health Inspector's Report relating to a house at 8, Spring Hill, Normacot. It illustrates some of the degradation and misery which JRH hoped to alleviate.

"A wife and two children, aged four and two, were in the house. The children were almost naked; the girl wearing only a skirt. The other child was sitting on a sack in the corner of the room. The furniture consisted of two dirty mattresses, two chairs and a box on bricks, serving as a table. It was near to Christmas and the children were blue with cold. The husband earned twenty five shillings a week, but only brought ten shillings home; the rest was spent in the Public House, where his wages were paid." This practice was not uncommon, when the man's employer owned the public house and demanded that wages were paid in the bar. The report continued, "A few months previously, one child had lain dead in the house for a week, because the three shillings and fourpence needed for the burial was spent on drink. The father said that he was prepared to, 'Rot in jail.' He received a sentence of six months hard labour for his third offence of neglect. This would have included a sparse prison diet, and time on the dreaded treadmill, which at Stafford had very narrow steps!

Hutchinson faced a real battle in the real world; his endeavours were immediate. The parish began to vibrate with activities to interest, educate and involve as many people as possible. Bible classes, Guilds, a Glee Club, Sunday School classes for both children and adults were introduced and the Parish Magazine made its first appearance in 1880.

This man of immense energy and strength of character, did not just preach to the converted; he preached wherever he thought it necessary. The crowded 'courts', the streets, the many public houses, also heard his sermons. The effect of his strength of purpose on his 'flock' must have been electrifying, no-one could ignore JRH. A little girl called Harriet Warren, attended the Church School and embroidered a sampler of what she saw from the school window. She was born in 1842 and had five sisters and one brother, their ages ranged from eighteen years to nine months.

Sampler by Harriet Warren worked in fine wool and silk. It shows the Church before the addition of the North Aisle, Vestry and Porch.

K. Edwards
From Church Archive

A Diocesan letter of 16th June 1891, states, "The church accommodation is insufficient for the increasing population." The third Duke of Sutherland was aware of these matters, and also the need for new housing of a decent standard. In 1891, he proposed an enlargement to the church, to comprise a north aisle, a new vestry on the north side of the chancel, and a rebuilt porch. The architect was J. Lewis of Newcastle and H. & R. Inskip of Longton, were the builders. The completed work cost £1,600 and was, 'Defrayed by the most noble Duke.' Suddenly, the energy and dedication of JRH ended. All his work for the parish, the stress of overseeing the extensions to his beloved church, resulted in an early death at the age of forty-three, in January 1891.

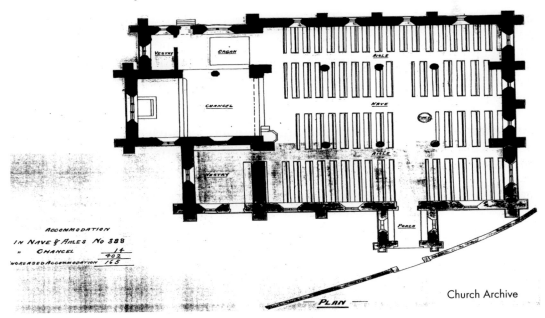

Church Archive

One month later, the Bishop of Lichfield dedicated the new north aisle and the full extent of Hutchinson's work could be appreciated. The parishioners then realised what strength of purpose had been shown on their behalf. With the death of Hutchinson, a new era began in Normacot.

The Church of the Holy Evangelists was to be guided into the twentieth century by another priest also possessing strength of character and firm ideas; namely, the Reverend Edwin Charles Hipkins M.A., B.C.L., who had been curate at St. James, Longton, for two years, until his appointment at Normacot in 1892. He served the parish most ably until his death in 1929.

There had been distinct influences of a Roman Catholic nature at Normacot before the arrival of Hipkins; the assistant curate Charles Frederick Godbold

Turner having been ordained in that faith. He left Normacot quite suddenly in 1892, the year of Hipkin's appointment!

Always thorough in his methods, Hipkins made sure that certain matters of which he did not approve were attended to in an almost ruthless manner. An aumbry was blocked up and vestments were destroyed. Some elderly residents say that as children they were told that robes and rich vestments were burned on the Vicarage lawn, by the Vicar himself. His predecessor, Hombersley, inspite of his selfless work for the parish and his early death, was denounced strongly in the first Sunday sermon by Hipkins, for his, 'inclinations!'

Reverend Hipkin's legal training and the discipline needed for his ecclesiastical calling resulted in many changes. The Band of Hope replaced the Temperance Guild of Godbold Turner; many groups were formed to interest and occupy parishioners of all ages. In 1898 the Mothers' Union was established as was a Womens' Guild and a Linen Guild. These had strong links with the Cottage Hospital and the provisions for a regular soup kitchen, both of which were a boon to the poor and needy in Normacot. A Girls' Friendly Society as well as Cubs, Brownies, Guides, and Scouts provided much needed activity for the young people. It is worthy of note that the Normacot Scouts have an unbroken record since their official formation in 1913.

*Normacot Scouts
First Summer
Camp Rhyl 1914
Commissioner
Wallace
Copeland is
Centre, 2nd row*

Bentley

Reverend Hipkins was not alone in his endeavours; his wife (nee Emily Jane Inskip Ramsdale) was unique in her service to the parish. Born in 1862, she was the daughter of Charles Ramsdale, the manager of Lloyds's Bank Longton. Emily worked selflessly, until her death, due to sheer exhaustion, in 1928. After her death her many duties were truly appreciated when a veritable, 'army' was recruited to keep the system working. She had been responsible for the Sunday School, training the Church choir, all the societies for the ladies and girls, the Mothers' Union and the distribution of the Parish Magazine. Interestingly, the Parish Magazine of 1974 contains an article of, 'Personal Recollections.' One of the items was by Mrs. E. Williams, (nee Hurst) who has given a lifetime of service to Normacot Church.

> *"She was a very small lady, but very big hearted. She helped the poor of the parish, begging for clothes and food and making up parcels to distribute to the poor and needy. She helped out many times as organist for funerals and weddings and often sang solos. My most vivid memory of Mrs. Hipkins was her love of dress. She always wore colourful clothes and lots of jewellery. Her hats were a sight to behold, flowery and feathery concoctions, with a veil falling over her face. I remember a tiny brown hat with a huge tangerine feather stuck up the back; what made it most amusing was that she always wore very high heels and as she tripped along, this feather would totter as she went."*

The plaque above the pulpit is in her memory, and describes her as "A Worker in God's Vineyard," but not, I am sure, in a dour or boring way. Her tiny brown hat and perhaps some of a more exotic design, would have enhanced parish trips into the nearby countryside, as well as excursions to the sea-side, which she arranged and organised. As Mrs. Williams said, "She was like a breath of fresh air!" Rev. Hipkins died in 1929 and his grave is to be found adjacent to the door of the priest's vestry.

The Reverend Hipkins, Mrs. Hipkins and their grandson at the Vicarage circa 1905

Walter Edwin Mountford was appointed as Hipkins successor in 1930. He was the first vicar I was aware of as a child and I liked him, as did all the other children. He came to the Infant and Junior Schools to teach us the Bible stories, how to behave in Church and the meanings of the parables, but always in a kindly way. When testing us on the Catechism, some children became upset when their memory failed; these were the stricter days of learning! Vicar Mountford would soon console them, sometimes taking them on his knee. In this way, most of us remembered what he had taught and looked forward to our next visit to Church. We were his special children.

Ellie, his sister, was equally kind and although far from robust in health, helped him in his pastoral work, so vital during the years of the Depression. Parishioners receiving monetary help from the Vicar, often suspected that the finance came from his stipend. The basis for some of his sermons and also for his mode of living was, 'I will not offer unto the Lord that which costs me nothing,' and he meant it!

Inspite of his quiet manner, small stature and natural humility, Mountford was a man of resolve; certain matters needed attention. He established an Electoral Register and re-introduced the annual Parish Council meetings which had not been held for nine years. Democracy was achieved when he made certain that ladies had equal voting rights in all parochial matters.

Sung Eucharist became a weekly event whilst numbers for Communion rose significantly; one hundred candidates were confirmed in 1930 and records show that this was an all-time achievement for Normacot.

Soon, rich new vestments, embroidered altar cloths and candles were in use at most services. Strangely, the services themselves were kept as plain as Hipkins had required them to be. There was no use of incense, no crossing oneself or genuflection apparent in the congregation. George Hurst, Church warden from 1948 - 57, and a life-long serving church member recalls two things which Mountford stressed. "With the plain service, there is more sincerity" and, "General confession is sufficient for our needs." The faith of the congregation at Normacot has survived many changes in ecclesiastical fashion and liturgy, during its one hundred and fifty years of worship.

To the Vicar of Normacot

CHURCH ELECTORAL ROLL

I, ...
(full Christian name and surname, Mr., Mrs. Miss)

of ....
(full postal address)

wish my name to be entered on the Church Electoral Roll of the Parish of THE HOLY EVANGELISTS, NORMACOT.

I am over the age of eighteen and am a member of the Church of England and do not belong to any religious body which is not in communion with the Church of England. I am not on the electoral roll of any other parish.

* (a) I live in Normacot Parish.
* (b) I live in the Parish of...
but for at least the last six months I have regularly attended public worship at Normacot Parish Church.
* Please cross out (a) or (b) : whichever does not apply.

Signed ....

I add the names of other members of my family who qualify for inclusion on the Church Electoral Roll of Normacot Parish and wish their names to be included. Please give full name. Also address if different from that given above.

....

....

A Wartime Wedding. Reverend Walter Edwin Mountford Centre

The Parish Magazine of November 1934 shows a busy month ahead, activities included a Military Whist Drive, a Camp fire Sing Song and a Re-union Dinner at the Dorothy Cafe, Longton, which was a prestigious venue for important occasions. There were visiting speakers, a Missionary Exhibition under the auspices of the Archbishop of Canterbury, who was, 'requesting' a ten per cent increase of monetary support for foreign missions.

There were two other items for November, 1934 which interested me. One was the coupling of 'Armistice Sunday' with the special day always held for Normacot Scouts. The troupe had lost so many of its members in the First World War, that this was deemed to be appropriate. The second item was the appointment, from the first of December, 1934 of the new headmaster of the Junior School, Mr. Robert William Eric Wilkinson, my father. He followed Mr. William Wilkinson, my grandfather, who was the headmaster for thirty-four years.

The Vicar continued to fulfil his calling through the difficult years of the second world war with dedication and devotion, but ill-health over took him and he resigned in 1945. He died, aged sixty-three, a short while later.

POST WAR YEARS AT NORMACOT CHURCH

Cecil Rupert Ollier M.A., became the fifth Vicar of Normacot in 1945 and was deemed to be the, 'Right man at the right time'. Young, good looking and energetic, he epitomised the feeling of new beginnings which swept the country and reached even our small world. Families were re-united and everyone hoped for a better and brighter future for both themselves and their children.

There was much work to be done. Parochial matters, church groups and pastoral care, all needed a special approach to cater for the needs and stresses experienced by many people during and after the war. Ollier coped with all this in a sensitive way on a day to day basis, until the greater part of the parish had settled down to a more ordered and predictable existence. Much forward planning was needed for the church's Centenary Celebrations in 1947; these were to last for a whole week. Ollier organised these with particular care and church and social events involved everyone who attended services as well as, those who were on the, 'fringe' of regular worship and parochial activity. Due to the success of the Centenary Celebrations higher attendances were recorded at services while Church clubs had renewed vigour and classes for confirmation were well attended. Ollier had a deep regard for church doctrine, in all its aspects and his method of teaching, particularly in confirmation classes, was a mixture of gentle humour, coupled with a reserve of knowledge which his pupils found both startling and refreshing; there were no dull moments!

Normacot Church circa 1950 and the E. C. Hipkins memorial pulpit.

The Old Vicarage (formerly Furnace Inn) was vacated in 1943 and a house directly opposite, on the corner of Belgrave Road and Normacot Road, was bought, initially, for Vicar Mountford, and then, was inherited by the Olliers. All the Church clubs, societies and whist drives, were well housed in the spacious rooms of the Old Vicarage, now called, 'Church House.'

Bowen

Mrs. Ruth Ollier inaugurated the, 'Young Wives Fellowship' which met on a weekday afternoon, finishing in time for mothers to meet their children from school. Discussions on a wide range of topics and visiting speakers helped to make the Fellowship a great success. The exchange of useful recipes, on a regular basis, was exceedingly popular. There were no T.V., cooks in those days and war-time ration books were still used for some items of food and clothing!

Cecil and Ruth Ollier's path at Normacot was not easy. Their beloved daughter, Cecily, died suddenly after a routine tonsil operation at Longton Cottage Hospital. Later, a son, Philip was born; he brought much happiness to the Vicar and his wife, and to the people of Normacot. However, inspite of his deep personal faith, privately, Cecil Ollier never really recovered from the loss of his daughter.

V.I.P's at the Annual Garden Party

Wilkinson

L to R. Cecil and Ruth Ollier, with Philip.
Mrs. McIlroy, Mr. Clarke McIlroy
Mrs. P. Millward, Mrs. G. Hurst, Mr. P. Millward, Church Warden

Due to ill-health, Father Ollier resigned his living in 1952; however, he continued to serve the church at Fauls, in Shropshire until 1954 and then in Narracort, Australia until 1957. After a short stay at the Queen Elizabeth Hospital, Birmingham as Chaplain he then became Vicar of Christ Church, Fenton for fifteen years from 1958 - 1973. He retired in 1978 from the living of Moreton Saye and then served in Kettering and Worcester before returning to Normacot as Assistant Curate in 1982. Here, he knew many people and felt very much at home, living close to the Church at 20, Ludwall Road. Although his advancing years brought the handicap of deafness, he fulfilled the duties required of him and achieved much in his pastoral care in the parish.

His sixty years as a priest was celebrated in 1997 at Normacot Church amongst the people who held him in high regard and with real affection. He died later that year on the 29th July. At his Funeral Mass, the Bishop of Stafford, Christopher Hill, officiated, assisted by the Rural Dean, Father John Pawson. The eulogy was given by the Reverend Prebendary H. F. Harper of Dresden, who since the resignation of Father Samuel Carter in 1994, has had charge of Normacot Parish as well as that of Dresden. On this occasion, the Church was filled to capacity. So many worshippers wished to take Communion, that both the High Altar and that of the Lady Chapel were needed.

On the 28th August 1997 a Requiem was held at Christ Church, Fenton, in memory of Cecil Ollier; the Bishop of Lichfield officiated and the Rural Dean, Father John Pawson, of Saint Francis Church, Meir Heath, gave the sermon. Parishioners who had received so many years of care from their priest were able to show their respect and appreciation in the presence of their bishop.

> Father Lawrence Williams B.A., held the living at Normacot from 1952 - 1964. He was an active and dedicated priest and the contents of the Parish Magazine during his incumbency bear witness to this. Church clubs, societies, whist drives and the annual Garden Party flourished. The quality of his monthly letters to the parish was outstanding. Although dealing with parochial matters, he often attempted to broaden the horizon of his readers, in the days when television news and wide-ranging discussions were not readily available in every house.

During Father Williams time at Normacot, the Parish Hall was built in the grounds of Church House. Measuring seventy feet by thirty feet, the timber building was erected by Mr. P. Millward, builder, of 259 Normacott Road. It was blessed by the Archdeacon of Stoke-on-Trent, the Venerable Percy Youell, on Advent Sunday 1956. and was opened officially at the Christmas Fair by Mr. T. E. Wild, china manufacturer, who revealed that when 'T. C.' Wild was a Church warden from 1921 - 31, a Church Hall was being discussed then!

Once matters were underway there was much enthusiastic support for this venture with the Christmas Fair realising £360. One hundred chairs were needed, costing twenty-five shillings each. When the Church Council met to discuss details, before the meeting was over, twenty-three chairs were already promised, whilst at the end of the service on the following Sunday, the congregation had promised a further sixty.

Not to be outdone by his parishioners, Father Williams organised a, 'Gift Day,' on November 3rd 1956. He was loaned a watchman's hut and brazier by the Corporation; he then sat on the pavement by the Church door from 9.00 a.m., until 5.00 p.m., realising over £107 from his endeavours. "Hardly a few minutes went by without some-one coming along with an offering," he said.

In January 1959, re statistics concerning the Church of England, he wrote, "Perhaps the most disturbing factor is the declining numerical strength of the clergy. But almost as disturbing, is the great gap that exists between the number of people who are confirmed and the number who make their Easter Communion. It is estimated that nine and a half million people are confirmed, but at Easter, the communicants are less than two and a half million."

He suggested that the cause was probably due to lack of parental encouragement and advocated a full family attendance at the 9.30 a.m. Sunday Service, which he hoped would improve matters, at least in Normacot. The accounts for December 31st 1958, show the scope of parish activities, as well as the monies available.

Accounts photostat 31.12.1958

WARDEN'S ACCOUNT, YEAR ENDING 31st DECEMBER, 1958

Here are the accounts for the year ending December 31st, 1958, which were presented to, and adopted by, the Annual Church Meeting.

RECEIPTS	£	s.	d.	PAYMENTS	£	s.	d.
To Alms	649	5	11	By Salary: Organist,			
„ S.S. Boxes	6	13	6	Verger	269	12	0
„ Harvest Supper	7	18	0	„ Church: Electricity	44	18	9
„ Salt Charity Interest	6	0	0	Fuel	92	15	0
„ Rent Stabling, etc.	35	12	0	„ Cleaning Materials,			
„ Flower Fund	15	17	9	Water & Laundry	14	16	0
„ Magazine: Sales and				„ Repairs, General	77	4	9
Advts.	53	6	1	„ Organ Maintenance	9	11	6
„ Fees, Weddings	45	5	0	„ Church House: Rates			
„ Gift, Old Scouts	3	0	0	and Heat Repairs,			
„ Gift, Pensioners	1	10	0	Light, and Water	47	11	7
„ Sundry	3	18	0	„ Insurances	17	14	2
„ Whist Drive	40	9	7	„ Altar Requisites	19	2	3
„ Dance, Shrovetide	48	1	3	„ Wine and Wafers	19	14	1
„ Dance, Old-Tyme	77	10	0	„ Printing & Stationery	34	18	0
„ Garden Party	195	14	7	„ Choir Outing and			
„ Churchyard Fund	20	0	0	Supper	25	5	0
„ Young People's Dances	18	0	0	„ S. School Outing and			
„ Christmass Fair	130	8	10	Party	56	17	10
				„ Vicarage: Rates, Light			
				Water and Repairs	73	19	4
				Telephone	30	11	3
				„ Dilapidations	79	18	2
				„ Cheque Book	1	0	0
				„ Diocesan Quota	106	0	0
				„ Magazine: Printing			
				and Inset	56	11	11
				„ Church Music	5	2	0
				„ Flowers, Altar, etc.	22	10	9
				„ Diocesan Stipends			
				Fund	50	0	0
				„ Sub. R.S.C.M.	2	0	0
				„ Zululand Mission	10	0	0
				„ St. Luke's Home	5	0	0
				„ Salt Charity	6	0	0
				„ Church Hall:			
				Electricity	52	10	5
				Insurance	14	0	3
				Flags	10	10	0
				„ Cottas	18	7	9
				„ Grass Cutter	12	0	0
				„ Piano	21	5	0
				„ Sundry	17	18	10
					1,325	7	4
				Surplus	33	3	2
	£1,358	**10**	**6**		**£1,358**	**10**	**6**

Compassion was never far from Father William's door; his two children, Mary Joy and Stephen, were adopted out of care and received a loving and stable childhood in Normacot. Humour, too, was never far away, as this inclusion of a true story in the Parish Magazine of 1959 illustrates.

Preaching vigorously, the parson came to the words, "So Adam said to Eve ..." Turning the page, he was horrified to discover that the final page was missing. As he shuffled through the other pages, he gained a little time by saying, "So Adam said to Eve ..." Then in a low voice, but one which the amplifying system carried to every part of the Church, he added, "There seems to be a leaf missing!"

The Wedding of Betty Eaton and Norman Wardle with Rev. Lawrence Williams.

Photograph given by B and G Wardle

In 1964, Lawrence Williams accepted the living of Palfrey, in the Walsall Deanery, followed by that of Stanton upon Hine Heath, leaving in 1980. His last incumbency was at Bettysfield, near Oswestry, from which he retired.

Father Duncan Leak, M.A., came to Normacot in 1964 and left in 1966. Whilst his incumbency was the shortest on record, his time at Normacot was appreciated and is still remembered. His work for the Scouts, which still have a proud and unbroken record, was outstanding. He extended and developed their activities to a degree which has not been matched since. Previously, he had served at a Mission in Mozambique and strengths learned there benefitted the Normacot Scouts.

A keen naturalist and a man of the out doors, he cycled for miles in the surrounding countryside, which was, and still is, both accessible and beautiful. Otherwise, his tall, powerful figure could be seen striding purposefully through the streets of Normacot when taking the Sacrament to those who were too ill to attend Church or when fulfilling his duty of pastoral care. This care is still remembered by some older residents as being, 'Real and sincere.' Many were sorry to see him leave because of family pressures. Duncan Leak became vicar of All Saints Church, Hanley, in 1968 and Rector of Swynnerton in 1971.

1967 saw the arrival of Christopher Martin Beaver, A.K.C., as Vicar of Normacot. As a priest, he always met the spiritual and pastoral needs of the parish. As a scholar, with a keen interest in history and heritage, he soon realised the quality and value of the Parish Magazine produced by Lawrence Williams. Each one had been printed and bound professionally and was a record of a way of life in Normacot which has since disappeared. His innate love of research resulted in his own excellent history of Normacot Church compiled in 1972 for the Diocesan Mission and Literature Committee and Normacot Parish Church Council.

The institution of Martin Beaver as Vicar of Normacot 1967 and Vicar's Warden, Donald Gray.

As an avid and knowledgeable philatelist, he encouraged many youngsters to become interested in his hobby. His own extensive collection contained stamps of interest and quality and included a Penny Black; his reputation as a lecturer of some authority on philately remains unabated. After

Photograph given by Mr. D. Gray

ten successful years, the Reverend Beaver left Normacot in 1977 where he is still remembered for the steady development of all aspects of church life and for his excellent pastoral care. He went to Pheasey in the Walsall Deanery, then to Doordon, in the Birmingham Diocese and finally to Lanley in the West Midlands, from where he retired in 1994.

Father Colin Lantsbery became the ninth Vicar of Normacot in 1977 and undertook the many duties required of him with enthusiasm and vigour. As one would expect, the Eucharist was the centre of his belief and in November 1979, the greater part of the Parish Magazine was devoted to different aspects of the Ceremony.

He had already introduced an evening service called 'Let Us Break Bread Together.' This he described as a series of "Looks at how the Eucharist has been celebrated by the People of God from the time of its institution by Our Lord." He stressed that this was not a, "Dry and academic study, but one which is essentially devotional. It provides us with a little more knowledge and understanding of how we come to be doing what we are today."

By all accounts, the evening services were a distinct success. However, the people of Normacot have always been cautious over what they deemed to be 'inclinations,' and Father Lantsbery also included a short article on 'Catholic Renewal in the Church of England.' Robert Runcie, Bishop of St. Alban's was about to become the next Archbishop of Canterbury, and according to Father Lantsbery's writings, was to be a, "Primate rooted in the Catholic spiritual traditions and conversant with social and theological issues". This whole article was well written and the ideas presented clearly, with the term 'Catholic' denoting the entire body of the Christian Church, but once again, there were, 'rumblings' amongst the faithful, who were working diligently to raise hard cash for the Restoration Fund, which was so essential to their Church.

The Guides raised £20 at a Social Evening; there was £20.65 from a raffle run by Church stalwarts of many years, Mrs. Day and Mrs. Edna Barry. A production of 'Brother Sun and Sister Moon' realised £25 and the Cubs did their part by donating £5.05. Womens' and Girls' Societies raised £20 and Mens' Groups £15. These achievements compare more than favourably with the monetary amounts for communions and collections for September AND October, 1979.

Date	Communions	Envelopes	Cash	TOTAL
23 Sept	82	£32.75	£13.91	44.66
30 Sept	98	£22.18	£44.13	66.31
07 Oct	81	£16.93	£18.15	35.08
14 Oct	118	£13.51	£27.83	41.34
				£189.39

As a priest, Father Lantsbery was regarded with respect because of his hard work, dedicated pastoral care and his tireless efforts to save the Infants' School. Changes in the Church generally, with the apparent leanings towards Rome and the increasingly, 'high' aspects of the services upset and unsettled many people, not only in Normacot. The changing from the King James version of the Bible increased the feeling of uncertainty for some and enraged others especially, when required to address God as, 'You.' Father Lantsbery's wide-ranging interest in comparative religion was evident when he quoted from the 'Buddist Wisdom Scriptures,' on the theme of the, 'Believing Mind' in a Parish Magazine of 1979.

> When we return to the root, we gain the meaning;
> When we pursue external objects, we lose the reason,
> The moment we are enlightened within
> We go beyond the voidness of the world confronting us.

When coupled with the building of an American Indian tepee in the grounds of Church House, many Normacot parishioners felt that they had much to consider.

In 1984, Father Lantsbery accepted the living of St. Mary and St. Chad, Sandford Hill, Longton, later moving to Cornwall, where he is now a deacon of the Orthodox Church.

DAYS OF TRANSITION AT NORMACOT

Appointed to the Church of the Holy Evangelists in 1984, Father Samuel Carter was possibly the last Vicar of Normacot. He was a young, energetic and dedicated priest with high ideals and under his guidance, societies and guilds for both young and old, flourished once again. From the new Vicarage, built in the grounds of the Old Furnace Inn, 'Father Sam' organised Church affairs efficiently in both ecclesiastical and financial spheres; renewed interest from the parishioners was his reward.

Normacot Church has always provided its worshippers with a sense of beauty, symmetry and tranquillity, but now under Sam Carter's care, the interior seemed to glow. The Church, was clean and tidy, even in its more remote corners. Brasses shone, the redecorated walls and ceiling enhanced the colour of the sandstone pillars, and the newly overhauled organ even had its display pipes silvered. Subsequently, the choir took on a new lease of life and reached higher standards than previously.

Decisive steps were taken with regard to the good use of certain parts of the Church. For example, the old choir Vestry became the Chapel of St. George, accommodating small groups for week-day Communion while the area adjacent to the font was transformed into a Chapel of Remembrance and was also used for personal confession.

However, national events were about to affect Normacot and many other parishes during the years of Carter's incumbency. Unwise investments by the Church Commissioners resulted in a massive fall in the value of assets. These financial difficulties now resolved, created problems for both priests and parishes. The Church of England hierarchy was confident that parishes would increase their giving; if this proved to be impossible, then inevitably the joining of parishes, the closure of some churches and a part-time priesthood could become a reality. As Dr. Wm. Westwood, the Bishop of Peterborough said of the Church at this time, "It is not lean and hungry; in many parts it is anorexic!"

Added to this, the suspension of all renewable livings was mooted and it was obvious that 'The job for life' even in the Church was not to be taken for granted. The world of market forces, natural wastage and performance assessment was here to stay. Even more radical change was about to take place because of the proposed ordination of women priests. From the start Father

Carter made his position clear and also the historical reasons for his subsequent decision, which affected Normacot so greatly. The great schism between East and West in 1048 occurred when the Bishop of Rome decided that his was the supreme office in the world church. So the Orthodox Church split, with the Eastern Churches comprising those of the Greek, Russian and Serbian. Quite simply, the Church was Orthodox long before it was Anglican, and the authority of the priest with regard to the administering of the Holy Sacrament, could not be refuted. On this basis, it was inevitable that some priests would leave the Church of England; Father Carter was one of these. His letter to the parish, written with regret, makes his reasons clear.

FROM THE VICARAGE

It has been my great joy and privilege. as a priest in the Church of England to know that my Orders can be traced back to the first Apostles whom Our Lord commissioned to lead the Church. There is nothing which can remove my priesthood, but I have made no secret of the fact that when the Church of England creates its first priestesses I will have to leave the Church of England. I will still be a priest, but the Church of England will no longer be a true Church following the teaching of Our Lord Himself.

It will be my first priority then to seek and enter a Church which is still following the Lord and intends to carry on doing so. This decision has not been taken lightly but in good conscience with the guidance of the Holy Spirit. I will be making myself homeless and penniless, but the Lord will provide and lead me into the Truth.

It would seem at the moment that I will be entering upon a pilgrimage to Orthodoxy rather than to Roman Catholicism. I would greatly value your prayers and support, as you will all have mine. I hope to stay until the end of June next year when I will be celebrating 20 years in the Sacred Ministry.

FR. SAM

Father Carter resigned the living at Normacot in 1994; in January 1996, I received the following letter from him, which is quoted in part:-

Please pray for the unworthy servant of God Samuel,who is to be ordained as a Deacon-Monk of the Holy Orthodox Church by His Grace Bishop Gabriel of Palmyra,Patriarchal Vicar for Western Europe.The Ordination will take place on Sun.21st Jan.1996 in London at the Antiochian Cathedral of St.George,1a,Redhill St.
On Sat.27th Jan.1996 Father Samuel will be ordained as priest in the Greek Orthodox Church in Paris.

Today, St., Michael's Antiochian Greek Orthodox Church at Audley, is the centre of Sam Carter's religious activities. Used previously as an Evangelical cen tre, it has been slowly transformed into a place of Orthodox Christian worship, with no grants, loans, or help from any source other than that given by his small congregation, some of whom followed him from Normacot. One can only respect the sincere belief of any priest who would leave the relative security of the established Church and step into a life full of temporal insecurity, to follow the spiritual path which he deemed to be true.

At present the Church of the Holy Evangelists is in the capable hands of the Reverend Prebendary H. F. Harper, the Vicar of Dresden. Now, the two churches built by the Duke of Sutherland are in the care of one priest. But what of the future? In the present climate it is unlikely that Normacot will have a priest of its own. There are no plans for the building of a new Church of England School to provide Christian teaching and the high moral and educational standards always associated with Church Schools.

The dedication of the Church at Normacot in those more certain days of 1847, saw the results of endeavour and planning by men of wealth and conscience. The Church has the wealth, even today. Will it have the conscience necessary to provide future guidance and stability for our young people, who seem to have no clear path through life nor, in some cases, even a passing knowledge of the teachings of Christ? As we approach the Millennium, with all its import for Christians, perhaps the hope of better things in Normacot will sustain us. If not, then John Buchan's concept of an atheist might at least cheer today's believers on their way!

"An atheist is a man who has no invisible means of support".

POSTSCRIPT 1998

On 21.10.1997 at about 3.45 p.m., young arsonists attacked the Church of the Holy Evangelists, Normacot.

The fire started under the door of the Priest's Vestry destroying the altar, chancel, organ, vestments and many commemorative banners. However all the silver vessels used for Holy Communion were undamaged.

A small part of the East Window was used as an entry point by the Fire Brigade because the fear of a 'fire-ball' explosion was too great for even a side door to be opened. Beyond the Chancel steps the main damage was due to smoke and water; this was extensive.

Roads near to the Church were blocked by police for several hours and at least three hoses were trained on the fire for most of that night. Smouldering rafters burst into flames again in the early hours of the morning; luckily there was no wind to aggravate an already dangerous situation.

Next morning I took a number of photographs of the dreadful damage done to a well loved Church. With a heavy heart I joined a group of parishioners who were talking together, some angrily, but all feeling a deep sense of loss. Each person had fond memories of the Church reaching back into childhood. The Rural Dean, Father Pawson and his wife had been in the Church grounds for some time and were ready to assist the Rev. Prebendary Father Harper who had charge of matters. However, the necessary official agencies had been contacted already and forensic officers were examining the interior of the building as we spoke!

One elderly gentleman was visibly upset when he saw the sky through the blackened rafters of the Chancel. "What are we going to do without a Church, a Priest or a Vicarage? Is this the end of it all?"

In the 'Staffordshire Evening Sentinel' of 22. 10. 1997 the Bishop of Stafford brought great comfort to the people of Normacot when he promised that, "The Church will be lovingly restored." This process has begun (1998) and is under the guidance of Father Harper who has kept the small congregation together with services held in the Church Hall. The Easter Communion of 1998 was most uplifting with a good congregation, hearty singing and positive prayers and thoughts for the future.

The Millennium is near and it is certain that the Church of the Holy Evangelists will be restored in time to celebrate this important stage in Christian history.

A 'reborn' Church with it's own Parish Priest and Vicarage would be a wonderful gift for the people of Normacot and surrounding areas in the twenty-first century.

We shall see . . . .

The East Window in memory of 'T. C.' Wild,
and the newly silvered pipes of the organ installed in 1892.

1994. Father Samuel Carter in the Lady Chapel which contains the Church's
original altar. Note the Stations of The Cross and the rich wood of the pews.

The author

Normacot Church.
The Morning After the Fire. 21.10.97

The author

The Priest's Vestry Door, Chancel roof and the twisted and
charred remains of the once silvered organ pipes.
The damaged grave of Rev. Hipkins is amongst the debris.

THE LONGTON MOSQUE, CHAPLIN ROAD

Founded just over sixteen years ago, the present mosque, which is based in the original Chaplin House of Dr. Heslin, shows the hard work and dedication of the Muslim community, their Priests and the General Committee. Much has been achieved since those early days, when the prayer room was housed in the ground floor room now used for the instruction of the boys.

A factory at the back of the building was purchased in 1993; this property faced Normacott Road, which was the ancient pathway to Lane End (Longton). Two years of hard work resulted in the demolition of the old factory, the clearing of the site and then the building of the fine extension which we see today.

Anyone visiting the Mosque is received with kindness and courtesy and all those who have a sincere interest are welcome, but should make prior arrangements with the, General Committee Chairman, Mr. Mohammed Akram.

Since 1995, the Mosque has fulfilled all the requirements needed by an active and thriving religious community, which has a strong and clear belief. Wonderful care is given to the Muslim children and much respect is shown to the elderly.

At the entrance, shoes and socks are left in the hall-way. The room to the immediate right is used for washing before worship or instruction; it is beautifully tiled, and has fixed stools for quite a number of people. On the other side of the entrance is the room where the deceased are brought to receive the necessary cleansing rituals and it is here that they are clothed in two white sheets before burial. It is clear that everyone is equal in death; even millionaires!

The Muslim religion requires burial to be as soon as is possible after death. However, many wish to be buried in their homeland, Pakistan, and obviously, special dispensation is granted for this extended journey. Because the local community is growing, with worshippers from Bangladesh and Turkey settling in the area, I understand that consideration is being given to establishing a Muslim burial ground in the City, at some time in the future.

The double doors facing the visitor lead to the large prayer room for boys. Two priests are in charge of the two classes and instruction lasts from 4.30 pm until 6.30 pm during which time, Classical Arabic is taught as well as the Koran. Further classes are held from 6.30 pm until 8.00 pm, and include special language teaching in Urdu, a knowledge of which is so essential when visiting relatives in their homeland and also to maintain the essentials, of their own culture.

The girls are taught separately in the next room, which is richly carpeted, as is the room for the boys. They receive the same teaching, but their room reveals the, 'feminine touch'. Many of their clothes are of beautiful colours and texture; I noticed that unlike the boys, the walls of the girls room are covered in pictures and texts, as well as examples of Arabic script. They even have the word, 'Goodbye', written over the exit door; Arabic and technicolour too!

All tuition is paid for by parents and the large number of children attending is a testimony to the support and encouragement given by their families. It was interesting to learn that there is no restriction on education, at any stage for the girls, as long as they live by and obey the teachings of the Koran. "A well educated mother would make sure that her children progressed in the world" was the view expressed.

The stairs leading from the hall-way to the upper floor are beautifully carpeted in deep crimson, and it occurred to me that only Westerners are foolish enough to walk on fine carpets in shoes or slippers! At the top of the staircase is a large landing leading to another instruction room, a room for the women and living accommodation for the resident priest. The remaining double doors lead into the prayer room itself, which is a truly beautiful room.

The walls of the prayer room are decorated in white and reflect light from the seven chandeliers, a number of which are individual gifts from worshippers. The specially woven crimson carpet extends the entire length and breadth of this impressive room.

Note the seven rows of identical pattern woven into the carpet (page 46). Within these rows is an 'arched' design in cream; each arch is large enough and shaped sufficiently, to serve as an individual prayer mat.

The focal point of the room is the Priest's Chair, or Mimber. This is a replica of that used by the Prophet (Peace be unto Him) when teaching. It is situated in a recess, or Mahrab, and is covered in a green cloth, green being the religious and therefore the national colour of Pakistan. As can be seen from the photographs, green is incorporated into the carpets and also the patterning of each window. The Priest's Chair is only used for special services, namely those held on the Holy Day, Friday, when verses of the Koran are read and then followed by a speech or sermon based on those verses, which is given by the Priest. When the chair is not in use, the Priest sits on a special rug directly in front of the Mimber.

Continued on Page 48

Mr. Manzoor Rabani with a class of boys

K. Edwards

The Prayer Room

K. Edwards

The girls' class with their Priest, Mr. Rasool Khalifa.

K. Edwards

The Priests of the Longton Mosque, Chaplin Road, Normacot
From Left to Right:
Mr. Manzoor Rabani,
Mr. Hafiz Siddiqui,
Mr. Hafiz Dil-Khurshid,
Mr. Rasool Khalifa

K. Edwards

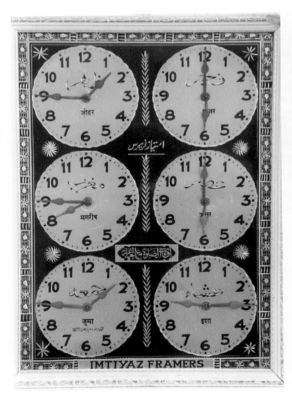

K. Edwards

Times for prayer. From right to left in each row. The clock face showing 1.45 pm relates to the time for Friday Prayer.

K. Edwards

The Story of the Great Mosque at Mecca, giving the Muslim Year and the Christian Year in each historical period.

The seven chandeliers enhance the rich colours of the carpet and bring a feeling of serenity and peace to a room which is so close to the busy life of Chaplin Road. This sense of peace is further enhanced by two large pictures on either side of the Mimber; a picture of the Tomb of the Prophet (Peace be unto Him), with its beautiful green dome and graceful minarets and a picture of the Great Mosque at Mecca, the holiest city of the Muslim world.

The Great Mosque contains the Ka'bah, or temple, into the north-east corner of which is built the sacred black stone revered by Muslim pilgrims. The Great Mosque also contains the well referred to in the Bible (Genesis Chapter 16) "And the Angel of the Lord found her by a fountain of water in the wilderness". The Koran tells of Abraham and his wife Hagar and their baby son, Ishmael, who needed water in this desert place. Looking for water, Hagar ran desperately between the two mountains on either side of them; she did this seven times. Then she saw that her son had drummed his heels on the ground so hard, that a spring gushed forth, providing water in abundance.

The photograph (bottom right previous page) shows the development of the Great Mosque from before recorded history to 1992 A.D., when the last extension was completed by the Custodian of the Two Holy Mosques, King Fahd bin Abdul-Aziz. Today, 100,000 people can pray there, together.

Muslims pray five times per day and in the small prayer room of the mosque in Normacot, these times are shown, as well as the time for the special Friday prayers. (Photograph bottom left previous page) They are calculated from sunrise each day and so are changing constantly. There are obvious difficulties for those who wish to pray whilst at work. Some employers are sympathetic to Muslim needs, but often a lunch break is used for prayer. If difficulties arise, it is permissible to have one period of time to include the five prayer sessions.

The Judaic, Christian and Muslim religions have the same, 'roots'. Jesus Christ is revered as a prophet, but not as the son of God and due respect is shown for the Virgin Mary. According to Muslim belief, the Prophet Mohammed is the last Prophet.

The Koran which was received in a series of revelations, had been recorded in writing before the Prophet's death, and many Muslims committed the whole Koran to memory, as they still do today. When I visited the mosque, one young boy was working hard to succeed at this task. He had two excellent mentors in the resident Priest, Mr. Hafiz Siddiqui and another Priest Mr. Hafiz Dil-Khurshid who know the Holy Koran from memory.

*The Resident Priest,
Mr. Hafiz Siddiqui
teaching the
Koran*

K. Edwards

The, 'surahs' or verses are sometimes difficult to follow for someone who is from another culture. Revelations of various dates and on different subjects are to be found together; for example, those of Medina are found in the surahs of Mecca. Early revelations are sometimes placed later, in the Holy Book, but the arrangement is certainly not haphazard; close study reveals a logical sequence and a deep significance. This is because the inspirations of the Prophet, (Peace be unto Him), progressed from INMOST things to those of an OUTWARD nature. Most people find their way from outward things to those within themselves.

During the last ten years of His life, the Prophet, (Peace be unto Him), destroyed idolatry in Arabia, raised women to the same legal status as men, stopped drunkenness and immorality amongst the tribes and established a love of faith, sincerity and honest dealing. For the first time in history, He made universal brotherhood a fact and a principle of common law. His support and guide in all that work was the Holy Koran.

As with the Prophet, (Peace be unto Him), so, with many of His followers in Normacot today. They work hard, they pray regularly and sincerely, they care for the children and respect the elderly. The Koran and the revelations contained therein, advise and guide on all aspects of life. To visit Mecca, at least once in one's lifetime, is the wish and hope of every Muslim and many work long hours and save hard to achieve this. As Mr. Suhail Akram was preparing for his second visit to Mecca in two years he said, "The Koran is an A to Z of living".

No one who has visited the mosque and met the priests and the community could disagree with such a true statement.

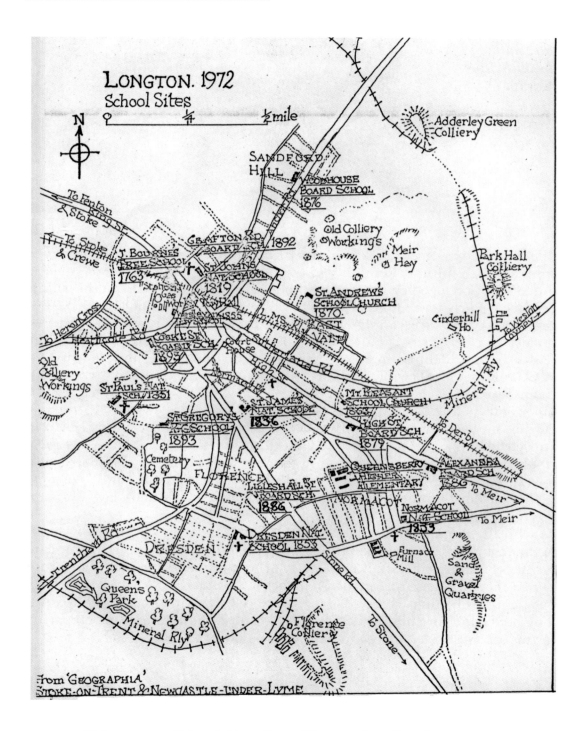

19th century School Sites from "Geographica" Stoke-on-Trent

NORMACOT CHURCH OF ENGLAND JUNIOR SCHOOL 1833 -1956

'IN THE BEGINNING' 1833 - 1902

In 1833, poverty, degradation and hopelessness were everyday factors in the lives of many children. Only education could rescue them from what had become, 'acceptable practices' and so bring some light into their bleak existence. This extract from Arnold Bennett's novel, 'Clayhanger' enables us to share the stark reality of life for a seven year old boy.

"It was the winter of 1835, January. At half past five that morning, Darius began his career in earnest. He was a 'mould-runner' for a 'muffin maker' ... The business of Darius was to run as hard as he could with the mould and a newly created plate adhering thereto, into the drying-stove. This 'stove' was a room lined with shelves and having a red hot stove and stove-pipe in the middle. As no man of seven could reach the upper shelves, a pair of steps was provided. ... If the soft clay of a new born plate was damaged, Darius was knocked down. .... Darius was (also) engaged in clay wedging. That is to say, he took a piece of raw clay weighing more than himself, cut it in two with a wire, raised one half above his head and crashed it down with all his force upon the other half, and he repeated this process until the clay was thoroughly soft and even in texture. ... Darius reached home at a quarter to nine, having eaten nothing but bread all day. Somehow, he lapsed into the child again. His mother took him on her knee, wrapped her sacking apron round his ragged clothes and cried over him, cried into his supper of porridge, undressed him and put him to bed. But he could not sleep easily, because he was afraid of being late the next morning."

This was the scene set in the commercial world surrounding the early years of the Normacot National School which opened in 1833. This building was licenced for services from 1835 until the Church of the Holy Evangelists was consecrated on July 23rd 1847 by John Lonsdale, Bishop of Lichfield. The school stood on the corner opposite to the church; it was replaced by another building in 1876 and two new classrooms were added in 1888. The former schoolrooms were occupied by the infants until their new school was built in Meir Road in 1895.

By 1863, it was established by national legislation that a child of nine could work for nine hours per day, and at the age of thirteen twelve hours per day was deemed acceptable. This was not so in the pottery industry, where these, 'improvements' only applied some thirty years later. Happily, for Normacot children, much endeavour, at least in school and at church, was made on their behalf.

All their classrooms were well heated by coal fires and on the 23rd November 1864, gas was piped into the school for lighting. From 1863 until 1876, the Headmaster is un-named, but his Log Book entries are interesting and varied. April 1st 1863, *"Two boys caned for bad behaviour in church"* and on April 21st *"Refused to admit a boy from Longton, aged eight. He was of dirty appearance and could not tell (say) his alphabet."* May 1st 1863, *"Children brought a quantity of Mayflowers to school; several children away with measles."*

THE 1870 EDUCATION ACT

Mr. A. H. Gregson was Headmaster from 1876 to 1887. He saw many of the results of the 1870 Act in his small school at Normacot and soon realised that it was the first positive step forward for universal education. Schooling was compulsory, but not free. 'School-pence' had to be found as well as slates, paper and books. The prevailing unstable economic conditions made these requirements difficult, sometimes impossible, for poor families.

The three 'R's' were of paramount importance for all the 'standards' from one to six, because the aim of the 1870 Act was that, "The working class should be literate." Under the guidance of Gregson, Normacot School prospered, numbers increased and the bond between church and school became even stronger. At the same time, the whole area became aware of the pressing need for education. Reference to the map showing 19th century schools reveals that the National School at St. James was built in 1836, Dresden in 1853, while St. John's, in Longton, was established as early as 1819.

Pre 1877, no child under nine years of age was allowed to work. Later, the Elementary School Act of 1877 stated that, "No child under ten should be allowed to go to work." However, there was an escape clause; if they had passed the requirements of the Second 'Standard' or if they had attended school two hundred and fifty times during the previous two years, then they could seek work. The requirements of the Second Standard were the, "reading of a narrative next in order after monosyllables in a school book," and to, "Copy a line of print in manuscript character," after which, the child must calculate, "A sum in simple addition or subtraction and know the multiplication table."

Gregson's Log Book for 1881 and 1882 shows the daily life of the school set in a framework of social difficulties. May 12th 1881. "Visit by the Vicar and Mark Knowles Esq., a Blackburn Temperance Advocate." May 16th 1881, "Payment of two monitors. Gave claim of fees for the pauper children to the Vicar for the Guardians."

To meet the requirements of the 1870 Act, there is evidence of regular testing in the three 'R's' and in May of that year, 152 children were tested, with a 37% pass rate. It is encouraging to note that a similar test in June for 130 children, resulted in an improved pass rate of 44.6%. One can only hope that the questions were not identical in both tests; it has been known!

On October 17th 1882, Gregson gave a successful, 'Object' lesson to Standard One, on 'Coal.' This type of lesson was a highly skilled method of imparting knowledge in the days of, 'Talk and Chalk.' Educational aids were unknown and the blackboard was central to all instruction; it was equivalent to the printed page or the computer window of today and information had to be presented clearly, concisely and accurately. The chalks were filed to a point, the blackboard ruler used for all headings and beautiful copper-plate script was the norm. The blackboard layout was usually prepared the previous day and then the teacher was free to hold the 'Object' and to show it to the children.

A TEACHER'S 'LOT?'

On 29th November 1882, Her Majesty's Inspector, Walter B. Yarde, visited the school without warning. Although the report on the accuracy of the Log Book, Admissions Book and the daily Registers was excellent (jobs could be lost if the Registers had one error!), he reported thus. "In each class, the Saviour's life was less well known than that of the Old Testament. Liturgical knowledge was scarcely up to the standard of a good school, but the general tone is very satisfactory. Attention must be given to ventilation. All the windows were closed and rooms excessively hot". At this time there were 56 children in Standard I!

Mr. Yarde departed and the Log Book reveals that a half-day holiday was arranged for the following afternoon; obviously acute areas of stress had to be remedied for staff and pupils as soon as was possible!

However, neither extra holidays nor unscheduled inspections could stop the. undoubted progress of Normacot School. By 1885 it had a capacity for 126 boys, 126 girls and accommodation for 155 infants. The actual numbers taught were in excess of these figures being 149, 153 and 178 respectively. Classes must have been large because Gregson's staff comprised Assistant Teacher Mr. Ford and two pupil teachers, Mr. E. Sutton and Mr. H. A. Wilson. The Headteacher of the girl's school, Miss Alice E. Morgan (1880-86), had four staff, Miss A. E. Hall, Assistant Teacher and pupil teachers, Misses E. Hallam, M. Meakin and M. Taylor. The Infant School Headmistress who was Mrs Rees, had Miss Robinson as her Assistant Teacher and pupil teacher Miss E. Hallam, who appears to have been on 'lease-lend' between the Junior and Infant Schools, which were on the same site.

"MUCH ENDEAVOUR AND THE WIDER VIEW"

Astley E. L. Kaye was appointed Headmaster in 1887. He was the first of all subsequent Headmasters of Normacot, to be a dedicated and active member of the North Staffordshire Association of the National Union of Teachers. Professional recognition was given to Mr. Kaye when he was appointed President of the Association in 1884, when after six years of existence the membership was fifty-six. Once again the Log Book reveals a rich and varied life in school.

January 12th 1887 "Promised a recognition to the teacher whose class passed the highest percentage at the next annual examination. On January 17th, the H. M. I. Report states that, *"The new classroom just completed supplied a want which has been felt for years. Both sets of offices, (toilets) are in bad condition."* February 28th *"This morning, Mr. Hombersley (Vicar) came in to consult about giving a half day holiday tomorrow, owing to the cutting of the first clod of the Jubilee Park"* (now Queen's Park.)

One incident recorded a month later on 29th March 1887 introduces us to Miss Ophelia Jane Hall, the redoubtable Girls' School Mistress, when, *"Mrs Dennis came to complain of Miss Hall threatening to thrash Joseph Dennis for taking a stone from one of the girls (who was going to throw it at him) and so frightening him from coming to school."*

Astley Kaye's wife, Sarah, who was a Certificated Teacher, joined the Normacot staff on the 9th January 1888 and by 1889 they were both able to see the beginning of great changes in education. The need for a Board of Education was already established and was implemented by 1900.

A wider outlook in educational matters was encouraged and each school could then develop individually within the national framework. Schooling was free by 1891. No, 'school-pence' were required and the leaving age was to be raised, by stages to twelve years, giving children a settled and lengthier school life. Drawing, singing and physical exercises were added to the curriculum.

With monies from both central government and the rates, School Boards were able to build new schools. The Church, which had established its own schools many years previously and which had a history of care long before 1870, now depended on voluntary efforts such as Bazaars, Sales of Work and Church collections, to continue education in the parish. The burden on the Church Schools at this time was great, inspite of some government grants being available.

Astley Kaye appears to have suffered sudden ill-health during 1896; no reason is given, but his Log Book entries are written in a shaky hand, so unlike the evenly spaced fine script of previous years.

The next Headmaster, Mr. Dogherty (1897 - 1901) collected money for Kaye's Testimonial in June 1897; unfortunately, he records that the collection had 'disappeared' from the school cupboard. Juvenile culprits were suspected, but no real proof was found. On January 4th 1898, he writes, "Mrs Kaye and (her son) Astley Kaye, Monitor are absent, owing to the death of Mr. Kaye."

Public health inadequacies affected Normacot School extensively in October 1897. Wide-spread diphtheria resulted in the closure of the school for one month; this was then extended for two more weeks and then for a further period until January 3rd 1898. Worried parents were still refusing to send their children to school by February 8th because the diphtheria epidemic was joined by an exceptionally severe outbreak of measles. The Log Book for January 3rd 1898 reads, *"Several boys have gone to the Rough Close school in preference to running about the streets during the epidemic,"* proving that in Normacot, at least, both parents and children realised that education and knowledge were their only hope of a better future.

During Dogherty's years as Headmaster, standards improved steadily; one important factor was the increase in Trained Certificated Teachers on the staff. By 1900, records show that there were no Pupil Teachers or Monitors at the school. Inevitably, this state of affairs could not last, but assistants Mr. J. W. Grosvenor and Mrs. Sarah Kaye were fully qualified to teach the 170 boys in their care. Again, records show the school battling to achieve good scholastic standards, while the hazards of 'real life' such as lack of stock, school repairs which dragged on, and missing children, were ever present factors.
September 3rd 1897, *"Arthur Starkey, Standard IV, has been missing from his home for a week. There is no known reason for his absence."* April 26th 1899, *"The yard paving has taken three weeks and the bringing of dirt into the school is finished. The boys now assemble in something like style."* October 4th 1899. *"Samson Bridgwood, Standard IV was caught above the eye by a swinging door at the baths (Longton), and thrown into the water and unable to swim. Mr. Grosvenor, the teacher in charge, while fully dressed plunged in and rescued him."*

The firm educational framework established nationally in 1889 and 1891 resulted in many improvements and also gave much impetus to the teaching profession as a whole. School numbers were rising everywhere, a wider curriculum was demanded and by 1900, teachers began to feel that their profession could well have substance and standing. The membership of the North Staffordshire Teachers Association had reached new heights and now numbered 387. No-one could have guessed that in the next sixty years the number of City teachers recruited would reach 2,500! At the turn of the century, teachers and pupils were aware that the years ahead would bring many changes to communities throughout the country. The stage was well and truly set for the next scene.

The Girls of Normacot School 1899.

A high level of parental care is evident in this early photograph

The End of the Boer War. 1902

With the new peace came the Balfour Education Act and the teaching profession realised that at last, a Government had made its first attempt to unify the education system. School Boards disappeared and all expenses were met by the new Education Committees.

Board Schools became Council Schools and the Churches were only required to maintain the fabric of their school property. However, this was found to be an increasing responsibility due to the age of most of their schools; Normacot was no exception. Log Books show that a significant number of boys went to the new Board School; four on one day and eleven on the next day. "Attendance is anything but good owing to the unsettled feeling with regard to the new schools," wrote Mr. Wilkinson, the recently appointed headmaster.

On a distinctly commercial note, Endowed Grammar Schools received substantial government grants if they agreed to accept an annual intake of 25% free places for talented pupils on a Scholarship basis. Before 1902, free places worked out at four or five per thousand. At last, it was possible for a child of working-class parents to progress from Standard One to university, if he or she had the necessary academic ability. The inevitability of leaving for the work place after progressing in the classes of the 'all through school' was no-more.

Elementary education was no longer an end in itself.

Mr. William Wilkinson and Staff
Circa 1904
L to R Standing:
Mr. John Colclough,
Mrs. Mary Wilkinson,
?
Seated:
Mrs. Sarah Kaye,
Wm. Wilkinson,
Mr. A. Brander
Monitor: Astley Kaye

Wilkinson

Until 1880, there was one mixed Junior School under a headmaster. From 1880 until 1924, the boys and girls were organised separately, each with its own head teacher; the boys were taught upstairs and the girls downstairs. "Segregation was serious," said one elderly parishioner. "It was a brave boy who put even a toe over the white dividing line as we marched through the main entrance!" From 1924 the two schools were amalgamated. Unfortunately, the Log Books for the greater part of Mr. Wm. Wilkinson's professional career appear to be missing at the time of writing, (1998). Wm. Wilkinson served the school as Headmaster for thirty-three years, receiving recognition from the Bishop of Lichfield after twenty-five years and again on his retirement in 1934. This recognition took the form of letters of appreciation and a number of handsomely bound books which are still in the possession of the Wilkinson family.

Maypole Dance,
'The Spider's Web' from
Wm Wilkinson's, Book
of Maypole Exercises
Circa 1906

Six headmistresses gave worthy service to the girls of the parish and to the raising of standards in local education during the years when the schools were organised separately. They were Miss Alice E. Morgan (1880 - 86), Miss O. J . Hall (1886 - 1905), Miss Mary A. Hall (1905 - 1910), Miss Alice West (1910 - 1917), Miss L. Morrall (1919 - 1920), Mrs. L. Tams (nee Lester) temporary (1919 - 1920), Miss Lilian Agnes Birks temporary (1920) and Miss L. Morrall (1920 - 1924).

Although Normacot was essentially a village school, it had to play its part in the wider schemes of things, both locally and nationally. Inevitably, these ladies saw many changes during their years of service.

Federation of the City 1910

Alice West (1910 - 17) was Headmistress in the year of Federation of the Five Towns and would have come into contact with the first Director of Education for Stoke-on-Trent, Dr. W. Ludford Freeman. Appointed in 1912 he visited many schools in the area during his first year in office making everyone aware that all City children had the same opportunities available to them. The Education Department occupied offices in the Victoria Hall, Hanley, and from the beginning, officers were readily accessible to teachers and their Union representative. This sense of co-operation between the class teacher and their employers continued until the City lost its Unitary Status, when executive power was transferred to Stafford. In 1912, Dr. Freeman established six education sub-committees, including a special one for school canteens and the monitoring of food for needy children.

As well as the three 'R's' the curriculum now offered Grammar, in the higher classes, the History of England, Geography, Drawing, Singing, Physical Exercises, albeit of the army drill style, as well as Nature Study and lessons in personal hygiene.

In 1910, under the single Education Committee, a Headmaster's salary was £160 per annum rising to £180 for a school of over 200 pupils; on the same basis, that of a Headmistress was £100 rising to £110 per annum. A certified male teacher received £80 - £150 per annum and a certified female teacher, £70 - £130, according to their position on, the salary scale. It took sixteen years to reach the maximum and equal pay was on no-ones agenda!

The Log Books of the Girls' School are detailed and also reveal the character of the individual Headmistresses.

Miss O. J. Hall (1886 - 1905) possessed a strong character; and 'opposition' to her ideas was not even considered. A highly intelligent lady with wide ranging views, even her changing moods are well documented. She is the only Head-mistress to use the exclamation mark in any of the official Log Books, coupled with heavy, thick script, which became more pronounced as emotions developed.

The beginning of 1900 saw a measles epidemic as well as serious overcrowding with an influx of 21 infants. Miss Hall 'drafted them back to the Infants' School.' September 6th 1901 she writes *"Changed Friday routine. I wanted the children to study the poisonous plants in the lanes. Closed school in the afternoon."* September 18th 1901 *"I took 45 upper girls to the, 'Menagerie'. A special lesson was given for the benefit of children attending."* On the next day, undaunted and no doubt full of energy, *"I gave a lesson to the Sixth Standard on Decimal Coinage."*

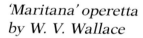
'Maritana' operetta by W. V. Wallace

Bentley

The Normacot National Girls' School gave a special performance for the Parish Church Dedication Festival in 1902. Headmistress and Producer Miss O. J. Hall, in her magnificent hat (standing right). Picture taken at the junction of Ludwall and Meir Road from the Bentley Collection. Mrs L. M. Bentley Front Row second right.

Logbook 1903 May 1st: "The new Education Act (Balfour) comes into operation in this Borough, today." Miss Hall obviously intended to use every relevant part of the Act for the benefit of her school. On May 11th 1903, she wrote "Sent a list of materials needed for school to Mr. Cope (Education Dept.,) I am practically without stock for working. I am still without books ordered by the H. M. I. (Inspector.) Mr. Cope indicated by letter that, "The School Managers must provide, until the schools are formally taken over."

Miss Hall's battle with Mr. Cope continued; neither one giving an inch. "Mr. Cope, stores sub-committee, passed my requisition sheet on the understanding that I make an effort to save the amount on my further requisitions." 1904 12th December "Letter to Mr. Cope complaining about the QUALITY of materials supplied and the IRREGULARITY of the orders reaching me. They arrive in 'penny numbers'. Here the script, underlining and punctuation marks show Miss Hall's true feelings.

Gradually, the Balfour Act of 1902 resulted in a 'tightening up' in many areas of school life. Attendance sheets had to be sent to the Education Office each week; every school had an official name and number. 'Normacot National School Number 8.' While Fire Drill several times a year was compulsory. There is much evidence that the Reports by H. M. I's and Diocesan Inspectors were becoming more detailed and wide ranging. The imparting of knowledge and the appreciation of teaching skills leading to intelligent learning, rather than learning by rote were being noticed and noted in every Report.

Miss Hall, had already implemented this new approach and for a number of years had trained her monitors to attempt, if not always to succeed, in improving their teaching skills to avoid excessive repetitive learning.

When Miss Alice West became the Girls' School Headmistress, (1910 - 1917) a whole new atmosphere of gentleness and calmness is apparent in the daily 'happenings'. Her writing is neat and precise as she reports that in September 1910, forty girls attended the 'Dahlia Show' in Longton and in October even Mr. Cope is pleased to supply nine sets of new reading books and has also obtained an extra stock allowance for the next term!

Dire need was experienced by the children during the Coal Strike of 1912. Miss West reports on March 27th *"More than fifty girls were provided with breakfast and dinner each day since March 15th. The Strike is now over."*

Inspite of the ever present social needs being met by the parish and the school, academic standards were improving constantly. The curriculum now included cane weaving, clay modelling and Fancy Needlework, with the new inspectorate beginning to visit, advise and encourage the teachers in their extended responsibilities. The Director of Education, Dr. W. L. Freeman visited the school on 1st September 1912. His four page report heralded a new era of knowledgeable and professional findings on the work achieved. 'Independent thought' was noted in Geography and History. In Drawing, the "Natural objects supplied were too difficult." He also suggested that some pupils could take intelligent responsibility to. "Correct and improve their own work." He summed up by saying, "The Headmistress (Miss West) was deeply interested in the welfare of the children. She is quiet, effective and in control."

1918 The War to End all Wars

The Fisher Education Act of 1918 established a further unified step forward for education. The Burnham Committee was set up to be responsible for teachers' salaries and two hundred State Scholarships were available by competitive examination. Stoke-on-Trent, under the guidance of Dr. Freeman, was one of the first authorities to set up Day Continuation Centres providing instruction for two and a half days per week, but the envisaged leaving age of fourteen was not realised until 1924 due to years of national financial stringency. Young children who had seen their fathers return from the trenches still lice-ridden and unable to talk of the horrors of war, needed stability. Nursery education was recognised as having great importance and the local School Board led the way.

'Smiles, Toys and a Maypole'
Circa 1914
Infants at the new Board School,
Queensberry
Teacher: Mrs. Boon, who was
well known for her kindness to
the children in her care.

Picture given by Mr. L. Tranter

During the early years of the Fisher Act, Miss L. Morrall was Headmistress of the Girls' School (1917 - 1919). A lady of strong personality and wide ranging interests which included drama with the Stoke-on-Trent Repertory Theatre,

Shelton, she was much encouraged by these steps forward for teachers. During her second term of office (1920 - 24) her undoubted musical abilities resulted in the Normacot Girls' Choir winning the prestigious North Staffordshire Schools Competition, held at the Victoria Hall, Hanley.

'The Winning Choir' 1923
Test Piece:
'Where Corals Lie'. Elgar
Prize: £5 (Miss Morrall is
on the right).
Front Row 1st L. Florence
Hurst 1st R. Betty Fallowes
Fourth Row
2nd R. Jane Fallowes
3rd L. Winifred Bengry
5th L. Doreen Amor.

Photograph given by Mrs. Jane Tunnicliffe

Log Book details include the Local Education Authority's 'National Baby Week' 1917 "Miss Sutton, who is a qualified nurse, washed a baby lent by one of the mothers in the presence of Standards IV, V, VI and VII girls." On April 9th 1919, "Avice Clarke, Standard VII, won the Essay Prize given by the City Authority on, 'A description of Longton Park.' and on May 15th, Mr. B. Craven, a lecturer of the Lancashire and Cheshire Band of Hope and Temperance Union spoke on the subject of, 'Eating and Drinking." July 24th 1919, "An extra weeks holiday granted by the King's desire to celebrate Victory." For the greater part of December 1919, the school was closed because of the serious influenza epidemic which swept the country killing hundreds of people after the first World War.

Miss Morrall developed the requirements of the wider curriculum in every possible way and in 1921 earned the praise from a Government Inspector as being "energetic and with high ideals." In September of that year she writes, "Have experimented with sectionalising Standard I." This created small groups of similar ability within a larger class unit and was a relatively modern innovation. From 1923 onwards, much support is given to the school by visiting supervisors; Miss Moulson (Girls Physical Training) and Mr. Turnock (Singing). The two schools were amalgamated in 1924 under one Headmaster, Mr. Wm. Wilkinson and was known as Normacot Junior Mixed School.

In those days of strict discipline, young Stuart Thomas Mountford and a trusted friend decided to organise a 'wider experience' for the girls! *"We set light to paper boats and floated them from the boys toilets so they arrived under the girls toilet seats".* Screams ensued and the punishment remembered clearly for seventy years, was severe! *"But I enjoyed school and had affection and respect for all my teachers, especially for Miss Lester who gave us a bar of chocolate on a Friday afternoon."*

'The Champion Football Team'
Circa 1923.
Teacher: Mr. John Colcough
The dreaded 'Iron Staircase' is to
the right.

The Haddow Report 1926

William Wilkinson had seen many changes in education since his days at Saltley Training College, Birmingham (1891 - 93) where he won prizes in English, French and Principles of Teaching. However, none of these changes were more extensive than the ideas contained in the Haddow Report.

The forward thinking Stoke-on-Trent Education Authority was amongst the first to implement its provisions, one of which was the re-organisation of Elementary Schools into Senior Schools for children over eleven. Junior Schools now provided for pupils between the ages of seven and eleven. Although the class teacher was still responsible for the greater part of instruction, some specialisation began to appear in Needlework and Craft.

From this time, the Entrance Examination for free Grammar School places tended to become the goal in a highly competitive 'business' with surrounding schools. At Normacot, competition was of a high order, but the all-round development of the child was guarded. Classes were in age-groups, not in 'streams' of A, B or C and compared with the early 1920's lessons were less formal and stereotyped so giving a wider experience for each child.

'The Top Class'

Back Row L to R:
Ian Taylor, Eric Edwards, Alan Hammersley, Wilfrid Lowndes, Kenneth Wade, Jim Dennis, ?

Photograph given by Miss Mary Webb

3rd Row: Chell, May Copestake, ?, Marjorie Godson, ?, ?, ?
2nd Row: ?, ?, ?, ?, Peggy Bridgwood, ?, Lily Adams, ?
Front Row: Charles Webb, Eric Ash, Freddy Frost, Arthur Forester, Frank Wright, Bill Underhill

Pre-war Hopes for Progress

The Llandudno Conference of 1937, organised by Government Inspectors, had an immense impact on the teaching profession and achieved exciting results in the classroom almost immediately.

The Headmaster of Normacot, Mr. R. W. Eric Wilkinson (1934 - 1948) had attended the Conference and subsequently introduced many new experiences for the children. Nature Study, weaving on looms, woodwork and physical training, which replaced the old, 'drill' based on army exercises. The girls enjoyed folk and national dancing and, created their own 'free style' patterns for embroidery. Experience of colour, texture and imagination for each child was the order of the day.

The new Music Advisor to the City, Dr. Percy Young, visited the school and soon after, a choir was formed as well as a recorder band; percussion instruments of a simple nature were also introduced. Serious attempts were made to teach the children to read music in these activities.

'Free Art,' using individual easels, large brushes, sugar paper and Reeve's powder colours was popular with all the pupils. Experiments with abstract designs were encouraged and also the mixing of each child's own choice of colours. Potato printing on fabric and paper replaced 'stick printing' which resulted in geometric designs, and again, texture and colour were appreciated as never before.

The Puppet Theatre
1937
L to R
Edna Colclough,
Sheila Walker,
Violet Bengry
Josephine Hobson,
Stella Meigh

Craftwork was extended to include the making of 'papier mache' glove puppets, as well as designing and making their clothes. The building of a small puppet theatre was a unique experience, which culminated in the writing and performing of pupils own plays. These were of a simple nature based on Bible stories, History or Morality Plays, with Good always triumphing over Evil.

As can be seen from these photographs, the school was old, with painted brick walls, but the educational ideas were up to date and working well. The scholarship results were excellent, inspite of the extended curriculum and compared more than favourably with those of other schools in the district.

Photographs:
1937

Open Day -
Display of Art and
Craft.

The New Physical Training.

Group Learning.

Dancing Display on the Vicarage Lawn.

L to R Iris Bradburn, ?, Joyce Wyatt, Mary Webb, Jean Toft, Beryl Maskery, Doris Newbon, Ada Lawton.

1939 - 1945 War Time Again!

Once more, world events overtook the daily activities of Normacot Church of England School. During September 1939, full-time education across the country ceased while arrangements were made to meet the dire emergencies of war. The parents of Normacot, however, were incensed about their children missing lessons and school resumed as soon as was possible!

The school staff in January 1940 comprised the Headmaster Mr. R. W. E. Wilkinson, Trained Certificated Teacher (born 1903), Deputy Head Mr. J. V. Wylie Trained Certificated Teacher (born 1906), Mrs L. Ratcliffe, Uncertificated Teacher (born 1891), Mr. N. C. Cooke Trained Certificated Teacher (born 1913). Supply teachers were Mr. E. Dale B. A., Trained Certificated Teacher, (born 1907) and Mrs G. Hart Harvey, Uncertificated Teacher (born 1904). The school accommodated 236 children.

Mr. R. W. E. Wilkinson. 1945.

Williamson, Longton

Initially, the children attended war-time school on a 'shift-system.' Shelters were built in the boys' yard. They were virtually useless both in capacity and position, being too close to the two storey building which towered above them. Enemy bombing would have resulted in children and shelters disappearing under extensive rubble.

This problem was solved for some of the children, by Mrs. Parkes, whose daughter, Gladys, was a pupil at the school. She made the large cellar of her house, in Ludwall Road, available during air-raids. It was large and was made more comfortable by the supply of chairs, benches, sheets for the walls in case of dampness and also a storm lamp for courage! Songs were sung, stories told and of course, 'tables' were chanted, while every one waited for the all-clear.

From 1939 until the end of the war, the tall windows of the school were strengthened with muslin or strips of passe-partout, forming diamond patterns across the glass. Gas-masks were compulsory for both staff and pupils and had to be carried at all times. Schools closed before darkness fell because of the stringent 'black-out' precautions. Suddenly, the children realised that everything was changing. Their fathers were 'called-up' for service, unless they worked in the mines, older sisters joined the armed forces or became Land Girls and many mothers worked in the munitions factories. Some of the teachers enlisted, one of whom was Mr. William Wilkinson, Junior. He joined the Royal Tank Corps, saw service on 'D' Day, the Ardennes Campaign and in Germany, France and Holland.

Married female teachers were recalled to the schools and also took their turn at Air-Raid Duty and helping at First Aid classes. Until the implementation of the 1944 Education Act, female teachers left the professon on marriage.

In 1940 the whole fabric of life had changed drastically for the children of Normacot. Families were incomplete, evacuees from London and Liverpool were beginning to arrive, and had their own stories to tell. Everything was rationed both at home and at school; even the meagre equipment for the wider curriculum was cut severely. The great hopes for the, 'new education' were curtailed until England was safe once more.

However, Normacot School won through during the first years of the war. On 20th August 1940, Diocesan Inspector, Rev. J. G. Hamlet reported, "Let me offer my sincere congratulations to the staff and scholars on the splendid success recently attained in the Scholarship Examinations." Thirty-five pupils had succeeded in gaining a Grammar School place.

War- time Log Books record enemy aircraft flying to important targets in Liverpool and Manchester. Interruptions to the school day were numerous, but short lived. September 17th 1940 "Air raid warning siren 3.30 pm. All clear 3.45pm. The children went to the shelters splendidly." During the following months, the sirens sounded at least once more every day with the registers often being marked in the shelters. Inspite of these interruptions, school life proceeded in a positive way, implementing ideas from Conferences and incorporating directives from peace-time Education Acts. 4th March 1941, the log book states:

"A school garden has been started this week. The object is to grow more food in war -time."

'Digging for Victory'

Wilkinson

Even in war-time a degree of help in specialisation is apparent with visits from Education Supervisors giving support and new ideas to the teachers. 1st July 1940 "Miss Hislop visited this morning (Craft) Miss Clare, the Physical Training Supervisor, this afternoon". Of course, some things never change; the next afternoon saw a visit from Nurse Bartlam, weighing, measuring and searching for, 'nits!'

Diocesan Reports continued to be excellent, "The teaching given is first rate and I deem the children fortunate to avail themselves of it" 17th June 1940. In 1943, well into the difficulties and privations of war, the Vicar of Porthill says, "I was most favourably impressed by the general atmosphere ... it is one of the nicest schools I have visited."

From 1940 onwards, much endeavour was made to establish the work of the school in the eyes of the Local Authority. The annual Prize Day was graced not only by parents and managers, but by local councillors and representatives of the City Education Committee; such was the growing scholastic reputation of Normacot School.

In 1941, The War Effort was well supported during 'Warship Week' when a half day holiday was granted to City schools in appreciation of their work. In the 'Wings for Victory' week, Miss R. Lovatt, the School Savings Secretary, reported that the allotted target for Normacot School was £400 but £1,041 7s 6d had been saved that week. A wonderful result for a small school!

On the 10th July 1942 the Log Book records, "The school was closed this afternoon for the funeral of Mr. Wm Wilkinson, late Headmaster of the school (1901 - 1934) and School Manager." and on July 28th 1943, "The Deputy Headmaster, Mr. J. V. Wylie, left the school to take the post of Assistant Organiser of Youth to the Stoke-on-Trent Authority." A presentation and refreshments were provided; those attending were the Rev. Mountford, Mr. George Blair, Mr. George Dale, managers and staff. This was, "In recognition of his service to the school during the last fourteen years."

September 3rd 1943, *"There was a short service to commemorate the third anniversary of the outbreak of war" while on the 23rd November, the Headmaster, Eric Wilkinson, an officer in the 3rd North Staffordshire (Longton) Battalion of the Home Guard, records "I shall be absent from school all next week on a Home Guard Gas Course at Penrith. Miss R. Lovatt, first assistant is in charge of the school."*

The Butler Education Act 1944

Once again, the end of a World War was in sight and hope 'sprung eternal' in the hearts and minds of teachers throughout the country. The Butler Act replaced the Board of Education and introduced the Ministry of Education.

Impetus and importance was now ensured, because at its head was a Minister of the Crown, the Rt., Hon., Mr. R. A. Butler, the designer of the Act. Although the war was not over and the country was at a low ebb financially, most people wanted to improve their own education and that of their children. A brave, new world was in sight and everyone wished to be a successful part of it.

The school leaving age was raised to fifteen; a daily act of corporate worship was required by law and foreign languages were introduced into non-grammar schools. To the delight and amazement of teachers, new equipment, ranging from record players and radios, to teaching aids for craft, pottery, gymnastics, gradually made their way into the schools. As usual, it took longer for these to reach the primary sector, and Normacot Junior School had to wait its turn for quite some time. The Log Books make no mention of new equipment for at least three years.

Another aspect of the Butler Act was of statutory importance, namely the safety and adequacy of all school buildings. On this point, Normacot C of E School was found to be suspect. The Log Book entry for 26 October 1944 reads, "A small committee visited the school to inspect the building according to the requirements of the Education Act 1944. Apparently, this building in its present condition is inadequate." The Committee consisted of Mr. Wilson H. M. I., Rev. Carpenter, the Vicar of Normacot and Mr. Whitmore, Assistant Director of Education. No further reference was made to this state of affairs, but with hindsight, it was a warning of acute difficulties for the mid 1950's.

On the 11th May 1945, Eric Wilkinson wrote "A Victory Service was held in school today. This was followed by the singing of Patriotic Songs", and on the 7th June the log book states "There was a Victory Day Service in Church at which cards bearing the King's Message for Victory Day, were presented, one for each child. In the afternoon, the School assembled for the singing of Songs of the Allies."

Gradually, the village returned to peace time activities, gratefully, but not unscathed. Some fathers never returned from the war, others were wounded and struggled hard for a degree of normality in their lives. Log Book entry 15 April 1947, "Mr. Wm Wilkinson, T. C. T., commenced duty on the permanent staff today."

1947 -
'Where is everyone?'
asks Mr Eric Wilkinson.
Note the street light in
the middle of the road
and the church spire,
removed in 1951 because
of subsidence.

After having guided the school successfully for fourteen years, the last entry in the Log Book by the Headmaster Mr. R. W. E. Wilkinson on 30th September 1948, reads, "This is my last day as Headmaster of Normacot Church of England School. I shall start tomorrow as Head of the Abbey Hulton County Primary School." During the interim period, from the 1st October 1948 to November 3rd, Mr. Wm Wilkinson was in charge of the school.

During his teaching career RWEW served as Executive Member of the N.U.T., for the West Midlands (1956-1967) and spoke on Primary Education at national and inter-national conferences. His appointment as Chairman of the Union's Primary Advisory Committee also involved the Chairmanship of the prestigious Annual Education Conference and submitting data to the Plowden Committee.

'Commemorative Cup'

Presented to RWEW on his
retirement from the teaching
profession in 1968
by Mr. Kenneth Locker
and past pupils of
Normacot School.

K. Edwards

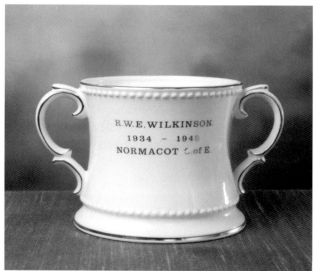

The School's Last Years in Normacot 1948 - 1950

A dedicated teacher and a man of wide educational interests, George Richard Donkin, the last Headmaster of Normacot, served the school with devotion and distinction in its final and most difficult years. He worked hard for its survival and during his first year at the school, endeavoured to expand the curriculum and allied activities.

The Log Book for 22.11.48 "The Music Supervisor, Mr. P. Rogers, visited this morning and inspected classes 4A and 3A in music. Miss Mary Webb took the classes." Encouraged by this support, on December 20th he wrote "The school gave a Christmas Concert at Queensberry Boys' School in aid of School Funds. The programme took the form of a Nativity Play, 'Holy Night' written by Miss E. Rowley and produced by Mr. Williams and Miss Rowley. The dressing was in the hands of Mrs. Ratcliffe and arrangements were carried out by Mr. Wm Wilkinson and the Headmaster. Miss Webb was responsible for all the musical arrangements."

In January 1949, fifty-nine pupils sat for the Preliminary Test for the City Scholarships. Prize Days, Sports Days, observation of the Feast Days of the Church, provided a busy schedule for the school. Increasing support from Education Organisers who realised the potential of the children included Miss G. Bryan (Assistant Music Organiser). Their encouragement gave stability to a dedicated teaching staff working in poor conditions. Enthusiasm still prevailed when on 11.1.49 "The whole school walked down to Sutherland Road, to see H.R.H., Princess Elizabeth as she passed by after visiting Paragon China." The next day, Miss Rowley took five children to the Queen's Hall, Burslem for the, 'Royal Concert' at which the Princess was present.

A Church without a Parish. 1950 - 56

16. 1. 1950, Mr. Donkin writes, "Noticing the worsening subsidence in the school building since the Christmas Holidays, I have today written to the school managers and acquainted them with conditions."

Matters moved quickly after Donkin's letter; a representative of the Coal Board visited on 18.1.1950 and a representative of the City Architect's Dept., on the 25th. By March 29th, the situation had become even more urgent; Mr. Garbett, H.M.I., and Mr. Salt of the City Architect's Dept., made a report on the building and a special meeting at their office was arranged for the same afternoon.

The next day, the Assistant Director of Education, Mr. Cawthorn visited, as did the City Architect and Education Dept., officials. All the pupils were dismissed in order that a final check-up of the mining subsidence could be assessed. Matters were left in abeyance for just over two weeks whilst reports were made to the relevant national and local committees.

On April 18th 1950, the Log Book reads, "The Ministry of Education, together with the City Education Authority, have decided that the present school building shall be closed, owing to mining subsidence. This morning, I have given the children instructions that they are to remain at home for the remainder of the week, while the furniture and equipment is transferred to the Old Longton High School in Trentham Road, our new temporary school. The children will continue to receive their milk and meals at Uttoxeter Road Junior School. We shall open school again at our new premises on Monday next, April 24th."

One can only imagine the upheaval experienced by staff, pupils and parents. The school had been close to the Church since 1833 and inspite of this exodus, the Log Book of April 28th reveals the fortitude and hope of everyone that all would be well, eventually. "Things have now become settled in our new building and both children and staff are delighted and happy in their new surroundings. Reverend C. R. Ollier took divine service this morning."

During the next two years all the activities and curriculum structures belonging to the previous school, were maintained and in some areas extended. The Annual Prize-giving was attended by 130 parents; it included awards for both academic subjects and points gained in the school sports. Nature Study was recognised with a prize for the best collection of wild flowers.
Outside visits included a performance of 'Toad of Toad Hall' by the Arena Players, Nature Rambles which introduced a study of topography and there was a visit to Longton Railway Station. The Normacot choir entered the Longton Schools Music Festival, held at the Central Hall, while 93 of them participated in an exhibition entitled, 'Church and the Community.' Excellence and adaption seemed to go hand in hand; 12.10.1950 "At the Harvest Festival the service was held in school with a large table serving as an altar."

Reports for this period indicate that the children were receiving education of a high order and that the Headmaster and his staff were supported by a large percentage of enthusiastic parents.

Accommodation for the 146 pupils was adequate, and inspectors noted that, "Much has been done by the staff to make the rooms bright and attractive."

Two difficulties were mentioned; firstly, the site was shared with older pupils from the Technical School and secondly the, "reluctance of some parents to allow children to travel one and a half miles" resulted in the numbers on roll falling steadily from 207 in November 1948 to 150 in September 1951.

The death knell of the school was beginning to sound in September 1953, when the Headmaster had difficulty in obtaining a teacher for the First Year. The staff was already reduced to two men and one lady teacher, therefore there was no needlework, games or physical education for the younger girls. Inspite of much attempted negotiation on 9.11.1953 it was decided that there was to be no addition to the staff and that was official! It is much to the credit of staff and pupils that a report by Jesse Howse, the Diocesan Inspector, in November 1954 contained the words that he was, 'very pleased' with the school. However, his deep concern and respect for a school with all the odds against it, was apparent.

Normacot Church Standing alone without a school

Lovatt

"I am concerned with its well-being, in as much as it seems to have little connection with its former existence in Normacot and is in danger of being dried up for want of a school to feed it. I do not know what can be done. It is still a church school, though controlled ... but it has no church life in which it can function. May I suggest that the Managers discuss this whole matter again and let Archdeacon Carpenter have any ideas which present themselves." Howse then apologised for using the report for material issues.

One year later, nothing had changed for the better. Once again, Jesse Howse submitted a caring and concerned report.

14. 11. 1955 "If this school could be transferred bodily to a site near to Normacot Church, the problem of its best self would be solved. . . . Away from its proper connections, it is difficult to supply from its own Infants' School and is in danger of losing ground, without any fault of its own. I hope that pressure may be brought to secure its return to its own parish. I hope that the Local Education Authority Managers will support me in this plea. The work going on is admirable."

Parents and Parish 1956

The Parish Magazine reveals the justifiable anger and bitterness of the thriving Parent Teacher Association, when in February 1956, an amalgamation with St. James School was proposed instead of the long hoped for new school in Normacot. A petition was prepared and signatures were given readily.

Extract from the Parish Magazine April 1956

PETITION FROM NORMACOT TO THE MINISTRY OF EDUCATION
The following petition, over a considerable number of signatures, will shortly be sent to the Ministry of Education: **WE THE UNDERSIGNED, RESIDENT IN THE PARISH OF NORMACOT, AND/OR MEMBERS OF THE "NORMACOT PARENT-TEACHERS' ASSOCIATION" OBJECT MOST STRONGLY TO THE PROPOSAL TO SIDETRACK THE PROMISE TO BUILD A CHURCH SCHOOL IN THIS PARISH BY TRANSFERRING THE CHILDREN ATTENDING NORMACOT CHURCH OF ENGLAND PRIMARY JUNIOR SCHOOL, AND WE URGE THE MINISTRY TO SEE THAT THE STOKE-ON-TRENT EDUCATION COMMITTEE KEEPS THIS PROMISE IN THE IMMEDIATE FUTURE.**

Jesse Howse, did his utmost within the restraints of a Diocesan Report, to alert those holding responsibility in the church and the City, to the parlous state reached by Normacot School, "through no fault of its own." One would assume that being 'responsible' would also involve an ongoing knowledge of real difficulties and some positive action being taken for the good of the community and its children. A suitable site in or near to the parish and a small, custom built school would have ensured Christian education and worship for Normacot well into the 21st century.

Unlike the 'Pied Piper' it was not realised that once the children had gone from the heart of the village, the future for much parish activity no longer existed. After a history of educational and social endeavour dating from the dark days of 1833, George Donkin's final page in the Log Book reads thus: "September 3rd 1956. The Normacot C of E Junior School is amalgamated with Longton C of E Primary Junior and Infants School as from today. The moving of the furniture and equipment will commence in a few days time. I, George Richard Donkin have been appointed Headmaster of the amalgamated schools. The staff consists of Mr. W. C. Williams (Deputy Head), Miss E. Rowley, who has been transferred to Longton C of E School together with Mrs. H. Stedman. On September 10th 1956, the scholars of the two schools joined and the Log Book for September 12th reads, "Removal Completed Today."

After 123 years of service to the Church and its Parish, Normacot C of E School no longer existed.

NORMACOT CHURCH OF ENGLAND INFANTS' SCHOOL 1833 -1983

"This Department is classed as 'Excellent', reported Government Inspector, E. B. Chartley Esq., in 1885; and so it remained throughout its 150 year history.

Initially, the infants shared the site opposite to the Church of the Holy Evangelists with the Junior School until a new, single storey building in Meir Road was erected entirely through public subscription in 1895.

A total of seven Headmistresses maintained high standards and helped to form a firm basis for the spiritual and educational needs of the parish and its children. All endeavoured to meet the requirements of successive Education Acts from 1870 onwards. However, the reality of ever present poverty, overcrowded homes and insanitary living conditions are reflected in the Log Book of Mrs Elizabeth Rees, the first Headmistress. She is well aware of the daily effort of small children walking to school, many of them being poorly clothed.

May 1st 1877. "Few attending school because of ringworm, whooping cough, fever and the very bad weather".

Absenteeism in July 1877 was due to the annual, 'treats' in the district. These were provided by the Non-Conformist Churches and required new dresses, suits and shoes so that the children could take part in the parades and outings with pride. Pennies, half-pennies and farthings were paid regularly to the Provident and Co-operative Societies to buy the outfits, which then became their, 'best' clothes for the rest of the year. On the great day, meals were provided, games were played and then the singing of hymns and solos took place. Generally, the music was of a high order, especially at Christ Church Methodist in Meir Road.

Often, Dr. Challinor's songs, written specially for children, were performed to good effect; one of the most popular being, 'Tell me the Stories of Jesus' which has been heard on several occasions during the 1990's in the television series, 'Songs of Praise'.

'School pence' were still needed in 1878 and on the 31st May, the actual amounts are recorded. "School Fees for the day are £1. 4s . 11d. On this occasion they were collected by the Rev. Hutchinson because of the extended absence of Mrs

Rees, due to fever in her house. By the 24th June, there is a heartfelt plea from the Vicar, "A small school this morning; I hope this is the last week of Mrs Rees' absence." The lady returned to school on July 1st!

His concern was understandable because staffing levels were critical. Children registered numbered 165 and the only teachers were Mrs Rees, Miss A. Wilson (Pupil Teacher 3rd Year) and Miss E. Jackson (Paid Monitor). Sometimes it was essential for the 'Babies Class' to borrow a Monitor from the Junior School.

Throughout her years at Normacot, Mrs Rees obtained favourable reports from Inspectors. 29 May 1879 "There is good discipline, with the children being creditably taught. Much effort is given to the teaching of private prayers." The celebration of Saints' Days, Feast Days and the Church Dedication celebrations feature regularly in the Log Books as does the strong connection with the Duke of Sutherland when Mrs Rees records a half-day holiday because of the visit of the Prince of Wales to Trentham in June 1879.

There is a distinct development in the style and content of her Log Book entries in July 1881. For the first time the curriculum is mentioned in the form of 'Object' lessons for the term, and subsequently for the year.

The subjects chosen are mundane by modern standards, but obviously began with familiar objects and progressed from there. 'Sugar, Flour, Tea, Coal and Honey" were studied first. Remembering that 'educational aids' consisted of blackboard and chalk, it is not surprising that Natural History was taught by the same method and introduced, 'Goose, Squirrel, Fox, Horse and Rabbit'. By October 1883, the Natural History goes beyond the day to day experience of the children when, 'Elephant, Camel, Parrot and Lion' are listed. No doubt the annual visit of the 'Menagerie' to Longton was drawing near!

Mrs Rees was systematic in her endeavours to widen the experience of the small children in her care. 'Varied Occupations' are next on her agenda and in 1885, these are linked with suitable sight-seeing. 'Hay Maker and Miller' to Lester's Farm, 'Engine Driver and Guard' to Normacot Station and 'Policeman' to the Police House at the junction of Meir Road and Spring Road.

In 1889, the Vicar gives her due praise on steady progress. "Inspite of dismal surroundings, she manages to keep her school in a high state of efficiency, although a few more desks are required." Numbers were increasing and the only staff were Annie Challinor (Assistant) with E. Lester and Angela Salt (3rd

Year Pupil Teachers). There was now a desperate need for a new infants' school because of the serious overcrowding on the original school site which housed three 'Departments' consisting of 158 Boys, 154 Girls and 156 Infants!

Mrs Rees retired in 1889 and was succeeded by Mrs Prudence Broadhurst who served as Headmistress until 1905.

A New Begining

Mrs Broadhurst had the unique opportunity of establishing the new Infants' School on the Meir Road site in 1895.

The air was fresh and clear, there were wonderful, unobstructed views to Cocknage and the Meir, while the new, single storey building was an unbelievable luxury after the cramped conditions on the shared site.

Page 10 of the Log Book for 1895 reads, "Present Infant School built and the old building demolished."

After two years, Reverend Hipkins realised that, "The staff of the Infants School should be at once strengthened to meet the regulations in the small print of Article 73 of the Code." Hipkins was a lawyer as well as a, 'Man of the Cloth' and his reference to the small print resulted in immediate help from the Education Authority in the form of £141. 4s. 9d for apparatus, an increase in staff and a revision of salaries!

1899 was a difficult year for Mrs Broadhurst. The school closed on February 6th for over three months due to virulent fever in the district; it closed again from July 14th to August 12th for the same reason. Her dedication to the school when her daughter died of fever in the following October, evoked official praise from Reverend Hipkins on the continuing good standard of work, inspite of bereavement.
It is worthy of note that every report until her retirement classed the school as, 'Excellent.'

In 1900, the Vicar was looking at the small print once again! Numbers on roll were increasing steadily and six assistants were needed urgently. Grant Aid of £162 for salaries was received, the Headmistress's award being £15 per annum. The end of the Boer War in 1902, brought the, 'new horizons' of the Balfour Act and once again, Normacot did well. Monetary help from the Board of Education resulted in the school receiving £137. Reverend Hipkins checked matters once more and in 1903 there was a Grant Aid, 'top up' of £200!

Mrs Broadhurst retired in 1905 knowing that a great deal had been achieved during her years at Normacot. She left a successful school for the next Headmistress to develop during the challenging years of the early twentieth century.

Ophelia Jane Hall brought a new 'wind of change' to the Infants' School as well as her valuable experience as Headmistress of the Junior Girls' School (1886-1905). Her first Log Book entry states, "I, Ophelia Jane Hall take charge of this school with the following staff: Edith Lester (Certificated Teacher), Arabella Jones (Assistant), Eliza Ferneyhough and Lucy Coxon (Monitors), Alice Rhodes (Supply Teacher), Ethel Hibbert (Candidate). Her second entry continues, "After one week's observations of the workings of this school, I propose to re-cast the timetable and to change most of the methods now used. I think more interesting ones will improve matters."

Miss Hall with Normacot Infants. Miss Edith Collett, her niece, is to the left of the picture.

Lovatt

Miss Hall aimed for excellence and usually achieved it. She was highly intelligent and a dedicated and knowledgeable teacher. In the Diocesan Report of 2. 11. 1905, H. Piggott Esq., writes, "The present Headmistress has set herself with great energy the task of raising the standard of work. Much has been done in a very short time. Methods are very good, the children are bright and interested. This school will soon reach a very high level of efficiency."

Meanwhile, Miss Hall continued her own weekly inspections and trained her staff to implement her methods of teaching. "I have advised the teacher of the Second Class to make the children rely on themselves more." This concept of education was far in advance of its time, a fact which was recognised in subsequent inspections. "Children of the top class attack the reading of a difficult book with confidence".

Such was the growing reputation of Miss Hall's 'Centre of Excellence' that Inspectors encouraged other Headteachers to visit from as far afield as Cobridge, Middleport and Grafton Road Schools to observe and learn from her advanced teaching methods.

Her Top Class in 1909 had to deal with spelling tests of a high order, 'Machine, Sieve, Chasm, Chaos, Centre, Heiress, Consequence, Science, Answered.' It is a moot point that after ninety years of free education whether or not top class infants of today could cope with these 'trip wires' of spelling!

At this time the Log Book shows participation in activities which have now disappeared. 24 May 1909 'Empire Day. I took the children down to the Square (A raised island between the Church and the School which in the days of little traffic could be used as an assembly point.) The National Anthem was sung by the three Departments and the health of the King was proposed by Mr. Wm Wilkinson, Headmaster." Three months later, on 27 August, "Children taken to Trentham this afternoon for the Marquis of Stafford's Birthday."

1920 saw the pinnacle of some of Miss Hall's ambitious concerts and plays. Each child must have enjoyed the opportunity of wearing special costumes and taking part in what must have been a word perfect production! Some children came from wealthy and influential families, as can be seen from the following programme, but in this school, equality reigned and everyone had the chance to succeed.

Programme of Concert 8th April 1920 reproduced on the following page

NORMACOT INFANTS SCHOOL. Principal Miss O. Hall
CONCERT. April 8th. 1920. by the Children.

- 0 - 0 - 0 - 0 -

1. OPENING...."A WELCOME" ......Miss Stella Beswick.
   ......Girls.
2. SONG...."Mollie's Bedtime"
   Miss Winifred Adams.
   Miss Marie Gerrard.
3. RECITATION..."Dolly's Christening"......Miss Jean Drakeford
4. HISTORICAL PLAY......"Joan of Arc"......
   Joan of Arc......Miss Betty Colton.
   Dauphin of France......Master Reg. Spencer.
   Master of Households.Master Ray Fallows.
   Knights. Master H. Boden, Master A. Dawson.

   LORDS & LADIES.
   ......Miss Stella Beswick.
   ......Master Tom Poole.
5. DUET......"No Sir"......Miss Stella Beswick.
   ......Master Geo. Dawson.
6. RECITATION..."Little Pat & the Parson"......
   ......Master Geo. Dawson.
7. PLAY......"Princess Marguerite's Choice"......
   Princess......Miss Alexa MacKay
   Undine......Miss Mary Kent
   Fairy Benevola......Miss Evelyn Tideswell
   Prince Innocent......Master Billy Davenport
   Prince Bell......Master Edw. Dale
   Prince Blondel......Master Bern. Bradshaw
   Prince Croesus......Master Arthur Little
   Knight of Sword......Master Ernest Boden.

CHAIRMAN. T.C. Wild Esq., of Blythe Bridge.

- 0 - 0 - 0 - 0 -

1. RECITATION......"Hullo"....Master Chas. Lovatt.
2. SONG........"Rendezvous". ......Boys & Girls.
   Shepherdess......Miss Ethel Jones.
   Shepherd......Master Arthur Little.
   Cupid......Master Alfred Dale.
3. RECITATION..."Flo's Letter"....Miss Marjory Amison.
4. HISTORICAL PLAY..."Burgess of Calais"
   Queen Phillipa......Miss Nora Sanderson.
   King......Master Geo. Dawson.
   Emissary......Master Chas. Lovatt.
   Lord Warrick......Master T. Poole.
   Lord Stafford......Master R. Wood.
   Six Citizens of Calais,
5. SONG ......"when I was a girl you know"
   Miss Alexa MacKay.
6. RECITATION......"The Cripple Boy"......Miss Nancy Brian.
7. PLAY......"To right the wrong"......
   King Conrad......Master Tom Poole.
   Princess Rosemarie.. Miss Stella Beswick.
   Fairies...
   Queen ......Miss Doreen Poole
   Sprites... Miss Marjory Amison (5 years old)
   Miss Jean Drakeford (4 years old)
   Appleblossom......Miss Molly Poole
   Hyacinth......Miss Winifred Bradshaw
   Crocus......Miss Margaret Salmon
   Snowdrop......Miss Eva Brown
   Violet......Ethel Jones
   Poppy......Hannah Gallimore
   GOBLIN KING......Master Charles Lovatt
   Goblins......Boys.

   "Goodnight"......Children.

I am indebted to Mrs. Nora Lovatt (nee Kent) for the following photographs from the J. A. Lovatt Collection 1920.

'The Fairy Queen and all the Fairy Court.'

Duet 'No Sir!'
Miss Stella Beswick
and
Master Thomas Poole.

'Princess Marguerite's Choice.'
L to R
Ernest Boden, Bernard Bradshaw, Edward Dale, ?, Billy Davenport, Alexa MacKay, Arthur Little, ?

Two future City Headmasters are in this group; Arthur Little and Ernest Boden. Edward Dale became Managing Director of Longton Transport.

Miss Hall retired in 1928 after twenty-three years as Headmistress of the Infants' School. Normacot must have deemed itself fortunate to have had such a dedicated and imaginative teacher in its midst.

Miss Elaine Cotterill was the fourth Headmistress and once again, the school had a lady possessing much strength of character to take it through the difficult days of the 1930's and the greater part of the Second World War. An ex-pupil, Betty Eaton remembers her as, "A large bespectacled lady with ginger hair. She wore flowery, calf-length dresses, or checked gingham cross-over creations. Her white pumps in summer and lace-up boots in the winter were a source of great interest to the Nursery Class who generally viewed the world from a lower level than the older pupils! In the summer, we always slept for a while after lunch and had longer play-times too. Miss Cotterill often joined in our circle games but not 'tick' or skipping; her build wouldn't have allowed it."

For years, there was a game called 'Rally-O' and Miss Cotterill was definitely not included in this activity! It consisted of two teams, male and female, and a 'den' for prisoners. The implications of one side taking prisoners was not obvious to the staff, but patently obvious to all the pupils. One day, at hometime I heard a somewhat disgruntled small boy ask my brother the sixty-four thousand dollar question, "Robert, why is it that YOU always get captured a lot?" There was no answer, just a faint smile!

Elaine Cotterill was unlike any of the other previous Headmistresses. She smoked heavily and drove a large grey convertible car which from time to time she attempted to sell to either Mr. J. V. Wylie or Mr. Eric Wilkinson at the Junior School. Needless to say, 'No deals were done.'

There are numerous memories of Miss Cotterill from 'ex-infants'. Apart from continuing the high standards of the school, she carried out the duties of washing clothes and drying them on the fire-guard of the big room in the true tradition of Infants' teachers. Gladys Parkes was fascinated by the large cat which was often draped round her shoulders as she marked the register or taught.

Edna Ridge, has clear memories of the First Class, "It was cosy, with its small chairs, tables and sandtrays. Everyone had a, 'Tidy-Box' made of cardboard with their name on the side. There was always a smell of milk, especially in the winter when the nearly frozen milk bottles were warmed round the fire guard. There were real straws too; they often leaked at the sides and the sharp edges cut your tongue if you licked them."

During the 1930's the outside toilets were still on the far side of the yard and had not been improved since 1895; they were best avoided in warm weather! However, for some, they are remembered with affection. The wooden seats, the sudden rush of water from the non-flushing system and the set of double seats were especially useful for continuing a conversation in some degree of privacy!

Alan Smith's memories reveal how huge the world and its demands can seem to small children. The loss of some arithmetic and spelling cards from his Tidy-Box resulted in much loss of sleep and maternal intervention was needed. His first day at school, though happy, saw his first breach of regulations. "At playtime, I strayed into a neighbouring garden, belonging to the Ballance family. No fence separated the two areas, because it had been removed to assist the war effort. I must have believed that the lawn, flowers and apple-trees were provided for the benefit of all the children. My lapse was soon reported and I was ushered into the awe-inspiring presence of Miss Cotterill, who had a reputation for severity, when it was required. No physical punishment ensued, but from that day onward, my cup was carried very level."

After guiding the school through the difficult days of the Second World War, Elaine Cotterill died suddenly in 1944. The Log Book entry by Rev. Mountford makes no mention of her illness, but records with sincerity, the sense of loss felt by the parents and children.

'Nursery Activities' Circa 1952

Bowen

When appointed Headmistress in January 1945, Marionne Fairs had served as a member of staff for a number of years and from the start, she brought knowledge, experience and dedication to her new post. She made sure that the school implemented the new ideas and standards required by the 1944 Education Act and always worked well with the Stoke-on-Trent Education Authority to meet these demands.

Miss Fairs was a quiet, self contained lady and her Log Book entries are neat, precise and almost understated, even when vital matters are entered. May 23rd 1946. "It has been decided that the Church will keep the schools." For the next thirty-five years this was to be a highly emotive issue for the children, parents and clergy of Normacot!

Many school activities were in the time-honoured mould of what is now a by-gone era. Miss Fairs maintained the observance of Saints' Days, Church Dedication, and the Christian Festivals of Christmas and Easter as well as the annual Garden Fete, with its Maypole Dancing, and the Rose Queen with her retinue. She regarded these strong links with the Church and the parish as the essential fabric in the lives of all the infants and guarded this relationship at all times.

However, the 'outside world' was changing and this school would be taken along new paths.

'Summer Play in the Nursery Class N.N.E.B., Teacher (standing) Margaret Reynolds

Bowen

The Log Book for the 8th June 1961 shows a degree of irritation over lack of money for essential staffing. "I attended the Course for Infant Teachers at the Mitchell Memorial Theatre. It was well organised and interesting, but did nothing to solve the problem of insufficient staff." The next month she records, "Open Day at Longton C of E Junior and Infants School. It is closing this term due to low numbers." The 'outside world' continues to invade the Log Book entry on 14. 12. 1961 "Survey by the Inland Revenue to assess the Rateable Value of this property. All Voluntary Schools will be subject to pay rates in 1963."

By the following June 4th, Miss Fairs is dead. She was taken ill on the train while returning from a short holiday in Llandudno. Some years later, tragedy struck the family once more! Her twin sister, Lilian, also a teacher at the school, was knocked down by a car at the junction of Eversley and Upper Normacot Roads.

A dedicated and caring member of the parish as chorister and organist, Lilian was of a delicate, almost fragile build. To the distress of her friends, she lingered for many days before her untimely death in hospital.

1963 saw the appointment of Miss Nancy Gosling as the penultimate Headmistress of Normacot Infants. She was an experienced teacher and had also served with distinction as Deputy Headteacher at Dresden C of E., Infants. However, the sudden demise of Marionne Fairs presented her with a situation which had to be addressed quickly.

Numbers on the roll had been falling rapidly; there were twenty children in the Nursery, which was more than the total in the rest of the school. This was not due to any mal-administration on the part of Miss Fairs; outside factors were to blame. The main one being the closure of the Junior School, it's removal to Trentham Road and unworthily, the fact that "Alexandra School did dinners!" to quote one young opportunist. The number of staff at the school had been less than in the days of Mrs. Broadhurst, namely the Headmistress, Miss Lilian Fairs and two N.N.E.B., Nursery Teachers.

The first school dinners were supplied by the Queensberry Road School Canteen on 6th November 1967 and fifty children stayed!

Nancy Gosling was as determined in her endeavour as any of her pre-decessors and with the help of Rev. Lawrence Williams prevented the closure of the school. Somehow, families were persuaded to enrol their children once again. The 'pull' of a Church School education has always been strong and surprisingly, this is what the Muslim parents preferred for their children. When discussing this point with some of the Muslim Community, it was clear that the moral standards and discipline of the school were held in high regard, the precepts of their own faith being taught at home and at classes in the Mosque.

Steady growth followed Nancy Gosling's hard work. The Log Book of September 1st 1965 shows 82 pupils enrolled and by June 1966 there were 95 children in the school while on her retirement in 1974 the numbers had reached 200. Many improvements had helped to revive interest amongst the parents. They included the removal of the air-raid shelters in the yard and the building of 'Porta-Cabins.' This allowed one class instead of two in the large assembly room. In October 1967 the tiny windows of the original building were replaced by large ones, ceilings were lowered and strip lighting was installed in all rooms.

Extra land at the rear of the school was investigated in the hope of using it as a play area, while the luxury of a central heating system as well as new flushing toilets which were approached via a covered way from the Nursery Room, ensured that at long last the latest, 'mod cons' were available for Normacot Infants.

'Waiting For Father Christmas.'

Mrs. Nancy Gosling (Right)

Picture given by Mrs. N. Gosling

With these achievements came renewed interest in a wider curriculum. Easels for art classes, with new paints and a specialist art cupboard for stock, soon led to displays in all the classrooms. Outdoor activities increased, educational visits were encouraged and the new Nature Table was kept well supplied by the pupils, as well as Father Leak, who often made cycling expeditions into the nearby countryside.

Nancy Gosling remembers the help she received from the Stoke-on-Trent Authority with gratitude. "Headteachers and class teachers could always, visit the Education Offices and talk to officials. We even had entree, by appointment, to the Chief Education Officer, Mr. Dibden."

When Nancy Gosling retired on August 2nd 1974, she could look back on a difficult and testing professional job which had been done well at a crucial stage in the history of Normacot C of E Infants' School.

The Last Headmistress

Appointed in 1974, Mrs Jean Forster's considerable professional experience and dedication to the school and it's children were used to good effect until the school closure in 1983.

When I spoke to her about the final years, she said "At the time of closure there were over 180 children on roll, six full time staff and an Asian language tutor, Mrs Norma Mufwoko, who taught one day per week. A secretary, caretaker, four kitchen staff plus playground staff completed the workforce. Surprisingly, in view of the closure, the school was listed as a Grade IV, had a thriving Parent Teacher Association and was one of the few schools to have a long waiting list. The Asian Community, wanted the school to continue because of its religious basis and its teaching of good moral standards."

The School Governors at this time were Councillors known and respected for their service to local people; Mrs Mary Bourne, John Wass, John Wallis and George Stevenson. So, what went wrong? The Log Books show that Mrs Forster had a keen eye for detail and an understanding of the rapidly changing world outside the school walls. Dealings with the Local Authority were businesslike, while contact with the parents understanding and helpful.

The children had an ever expanding curriculum and thereby new pursuits. The punishments book for 1974 to 1983 was completely empty, so the children must have felt secure, happy and motivated.

Jean Forster broadened each child's experience whenever possible. In May 1975, Longton Fire Brigade visited the school with their hoses, helmets and fire engine. Later that year Longton Police, with a patrol motorbike, gave a demonstration of road safety and community policing. The children who were already involved with all aspects of the 'Green Cross Code' were delighted by these visits and pictures and diaries were produced and displayed in school.

An Environmental Studies Course at Gladstone Pottery lasting nine weeks was a unique milestone in the school's history. The children were encouraged in the elements of 'own study' which grew naturally out of their observations and experience.

However, life outside the school was changing with 'break-ins' and theft of school property while matters of a potentially serious nature, are entered in November 1978, "Two men in a van enquired about a child in the Nursery. Social Services contacted immediately." Meanwhile, the rest of the year saw more break-ins to the mobile classrooms.

It is evident that the role of the school on a daily basis had to be re-examined when parents began to call for their children long after school-time had finished. "School hours are between 9.30 to 12.30 and 1.30 to 3.30. Some children are still at school at 4.30 and are often distressed. Also, I have had to ask parents to avoid parking their cars on the zig-zag lines outside the school gates." This was the beginning of an on-going problem which is still with us today!

Health and Safety awareness was beginning to be of real importance in schools and Jean Forster tackled matters efficiently. March 18 1976 "Unsuitable glass in the door at the far end of the hall; this is a busy area and the two long glass panels are three feet from the ground." Although the Authority pleaded lack of money, after further 'consultation' the matter was resolved early in May! A close watch was also kept on the new regulations of heating in schools and data was 'logged' when necessary.

Encouraging news was entered in 1978, "Notes on the new school are in the Manager's File." The Managers for 1977/78 being W. G. Wass Esq., Mrs. S. Perry, John Wallis Esq., and J. Mountford Esq. There were eight more people on the Parent Teacher Committee as well as the Headmistress, the Vice-Chairman Mrs. B. Taylor, Treasurer, Mrs. S. M. Harper and the Secretary, Mrs. M. C. Ernest. This committee organised fundraising events and the annual membership fee of 20p paid by nearly all the parents helped to keep the coffers full. Obviously, the parents and the parish were fully involved in the life of the school and it's future.

The only reference to the Diocese of Lichfield Education Council occurs in April 1978. A team of Diocesan Visitors, authorised by the Bishop to examine the role of the Church in school with regard to the 1944 Education Act, was headed by the Rev. Roger Vaughan. After the initial entry, no further mention is made of this 'venture'.

Perhaps in preparation for this visit, Jean Forster listed the dimensions of existing classrooms meticulously. When compared with more recent school building projects, they could be of interest today.

Class I (22' 2" x 19' 7"), Hall (45' 8" x 24' 8"), Nursery Room (21' 8" x 24' 4"), Top Classroom (12' 7" x 22' 4"), Nursery Cloakroom (10' 6" x 12'). The two Mobile Classrooms measured (24' x 24') and (30' x 18'). Other areas included the Staffroom (10' x 19') and the Office (9' x 12').

On August 31st 1981 matters moved swiftly when school closure was broached and a twelve months notice was then served by the Authority. An extra ordinary meeting was called by the parents in January 1982 and the Education Officer, Mr. King, was invited to attend.

Jean Forster recalled, "We were told that admission numbers throughout the City were falling; ours were excellent. Inspite of a massive petition from the parents and the Asian Community, nothing could be done. Father Lantsbery was tireless in his efforts to keep the Infants' School, but the Secretary of State approved the closure in March 1982. This appeared to be in line with the closure of a further twenty-nine schools in the City, some of them Church Schools. There was no turning back."

One can only guess at the sense of loss and the end of something wonderful, when on the 21st July 1983, at 1. 45 pm there was a special service for everyone at the Church of the Holy Evangelists. This was the final demise of the school which was founded by public subscription in 1895.

Those attending the service included civic dignitaries, architects, Inspectors of Religion from both the Education Authority and the Diocese. Parents and children packed the Church and the service was presided over by Rev. Colin Lantsbery. Each child received a prize. There were sixty-five 'New Testament Stories for Younger Children,' and the same number of 'The Good News Bible'. The Imam of the Longton Mosque presented 'The Elementary Teachings of Islam' to all the Asian children. (There is a full copy of the final service in Stafford Reference Library) Jean Forster said, "It was a wonderful afternoon followed by tea for everyone in the Church Hall."

However, after such an uplifting Church Service the events of the following day were demoralising for everyone.

The school piano was removed early in the day so the last children to occupy the school sang their hymns and songs unaccompanied. In addition, there was no electricity and no hot water available for the entire day and all documents which were not returnable to the Chief Education Officer at Stafford, had to be shredded. Finally, Jean Forster said goodbye to the children, parents and even grand-parents who had once attended the school themselves and had come on the 'last day.' Her final duty was to lock the school and then take the key to the Vicarage!

'The Grand Finale?'
The Cross of Christ against a darkening sky

The Author

THE SUTHERLAND INSTITUTE

'Longton's Temple of Learning'

The next time you walk past the Sutherland Institute, try to imagine you are part of a highly organised and excited crowd of 5,000 people lining a processional route. The date is the 7th January 1897 and the Prince of Wales is about to arrive to lay the Institute Foundation Stone. When considering the present day scene, with its somewhat alien pea-green metal bridge spanning the nearby A50 roadway, such a request might be difficult to achieve. So, how did it all begin in the more understandable world of 1897?

A subscription library of one thousand books was established in Longton, as early as 1807. By 1840, this was in the reliable hands of the Longton Athenaeum and Mechanics Institute formed for, 'mutual improvement' by the working men of Longton. They met in the Vauxhall Schoolroom, moving to Caroline Street in 1848, where one hundred and thirty members subscribed between ten shillings and one pound per annum, according to the facilities enjoyed. Circa 1849, they moved to what must have been a happy and relaxed venue, the 'Hare and Hounds' Public House, in Gower Street, Longton! This venture was initiated by G. E. Farmer Esq., (1837-1915) printer and stationer, and a group of fellow socialists. One of his daughters, Florence Farmer, became Lord Mayor of Stoke-on-Trent in 1931.

When the Borough adopted the Free Libraries Act of 1891, all books were transferred to Longton Town Hall, forming a lending library of nearly six thousand books. The Duke of Sutherland had already given seven hundred and thirty two volumes which were mainly historical and constitutional records of the sixteenth and seventeenth centuries. During his mayoral year, (1895-96) he inspected the existing library and saw the real need for a new and larger building. So, in January 1896, he presented a suitable site to the Borough for a new free library and technical school. He wished it to be built in Renaissance style using red brick and stone; any enrichments were to be of terracotta and the estimated cost was to

be in the region of £10,000. The Duke invited the Prince of Wales to lay the foundation stone on 7th January 1897. H. R. H., was the Most Worshipful Grand Master of the Masonic Brethren and in honour of his visit and the importance of the project itself, the Etruscan Lodge donated fifty guineas immediately. Prior to this, in November 1896, there had been an embarrassing public denunciation of Freemasonry by a member of the local literary society deeming it, 'A dangerous and secret association'. Inspite of this outburst, arrangements went ahead and what superb arrangements they were!

By order of the Council, the processional route and all the streets were to be decorated lavishly with crimson and gold bunting, but at a cost of no more than £300. The decorations began as far afield as the Queen's Park railway bridge in Trentham Road, where a richly decorated triumphal arch proclaimed, 'A Hearty Welcome to the Duke and his Royal Visitors.' This arch and its loyal message was repeated at the bottom of Trentham Road, Dresden and also at the entrance to the Queen's Theatre. The processional route passed along Stafford Street, the Market Place, Commerce Street, Stone Road and Rosslyn Road. Even the railway bridge at Longton Station was resplendent with evergreens and heraldic shields representing each borough. To complete the picture, the Corporation illuminated the Town Hall and Court House at a cost of ten pounds and undertook the fitting of gas jets to shopfronts for a nominal sum of money.

All the arrangements were efficient, detailed, imaginative and cost effective. Tenders were obtained for the marquee to house the ceremony, which was won by J. Lyons and Company Limited, of London. They provided seating for at least 2,000 people, with sufficient chairs in suitably arranged tiers. They were responsible for the numbering of seats, all tickets, furnishings for the Royal Dais, decorations, flags, palms and flowering plants. Exits and entrances were to be marked clearly while all steps were to be edged with white tape. Amazingly, the whole marquee was heated by gas chandeliers and stoves as the Council was well aware that the ceremony would take place in early January.

Additional arrangements included another marquee to house the Corporation Waiting Room and the Royal Vestibule. Toilet areas for both Royalty and Commoners taking part in the ceremony, were to be lined, draped and furnished. The arrangements were certainly efficient and definitely cost effective when one realises that all this was obtained for £540, including the services of a first class Hungarian Band in full regalia! The stage was now set for the Masonic Lodges and Municipal representatives to play their part in this unique ceremony.

The Municipal Procession was impressive by any standards. Preceded by the Mounted Police, the Longton Military Band and the first part of the Fire Brigade in open order, came the Borough Magistrates and Justices' Clerks. Next in procession were the Mayors of all the Potteries Towns and those of Newcastle and Stafford who were dressed in the robes and golden chains of office. Alderman Edwards, Mayor of Longton, was magnificent in robes of figured black silk, heavily embellished with gold lacing. The new Corporation robes for Longton, were of blue cloth with velvet trim, while councillors wore robes of blue cloth with fur trim. The Mayors of Newcastle and Stafford, Burslem and Stoke were resplendent in robes of scarlet and ermine. Dr. Davies, the Medical Officer for Longton wore his gown of plain blue silk, while the Town Clerk, G. C. Kent, Esq., wore morning dress. Others in the procession were men of merit and responsibility in the community; the Surveyor and the Accountant for the Borough, the Gas Manager, the Chaplain, the Borough Treasurer and Town Clerk and three Aldermen. The last in the procession were the second part of the Fire Brigade and the musicians of the Borough Band.

Meanwhile, the Masonic Brethren assembled at the Zion Methodist New Connection Chapel, donned their robes and then met at the Queen's Theatre. Here, they sang the National Anthem and 'God Bless the Prince of Wales' followed by a new anthem, 'God Bless Queen Victoria'. The Earl of Dartmouth presided over more than one thousand Brethren and it was agreed that an address of welcome would be given to the Prince at the beginning of the ceremony. They then re-assembled and marched along the processional route which was past the Court House at the end of Commerce Street, down Market Street, up Stafford Street to Stone Road. Mr. Wm. Finney, a stationer of London Road, Stoke, saw the whole parade and described the Masons as, "A magnificent spectacle in their gorgeous trappings and apparel. They trouped forward in one continuous stream."

The timing of the ceremony was perfect. Just as all were assembled, the Royal Party arrived from Trentham Hall in a closed carriage, because of the heavy rain. Nearly one thousand people had waited outside the marquee and inspite of being, 'soaked', raised a hearty cheer. The Guard of Honour, from the First Volunteer Battalion of the North Staffordshire Regiment, greeted the dignitaries and then Lord Dartmouth presented the Masonic Address, in the form of an heraldic scroll, prepared by Messrs., Hughes and Harber, of Longton. After the Mayoral welcome, the Prince and his party were escorted to the dais by the Duke of Sutherland and high ranking Masonic Officers. Three Masters of Lodges carried cornucopia and ewers containing wine and oil, while others of high Masonic status carried the plate with the foundation stone inscriptions, the plumb rule, square and mallet, and lastly, the Great Seal. The Duke of Sutherland then handed the deed of conveyance for the site to the Mayor, as a free gift to the people of Longton.

H.R.H.
The Prince of Wales

His Royal Highness laid the Foundation Stone, after which the Archdeacon of Essex led prayers of consecration. This large piece of Aberdeen stone was three feet in breadth, two feet high and rested on a plinth of local Hollington stone. It was set on brickwork reaching over thirteen feet below the floor-line and was set firmly in concrete. At the Prince's request, the Grand Treasurer placed the following items in the lower cavity; current coins of the realm from a sovereign downwards, copies of 'The Times,' the Staffordshire, 'Sentinel' and the, 'Longton Times and Echo.' The Prince then said, "May the blessings of morality and virtue flourish in this building, producing fruit one hundred fold". Afterwards, he poured wine over the stone for joy and gladness and oil as an emblem of peace.

The Borough Surveyor, Mr. J. W. Wardle, submitted the plans to the Prince, who duly returned them saying "I desire that you proceed without loss of time to the completion of the work, in conformity with the plans and designs now entrusted to you." This concluded the ceremony and purses were then presented to the Princess of Wales from the Masonic Lodges, pottery factories, manufacturers and schools. Miss E. Brunt presented a purse of £2. 10. 0 for Normacot Church of England Junior School and Miss Annie Wild presented £5. 5. 0 for T. C. Wild and Company.
When the Grand Officers conducted the Prince round the Pavilion there was much cheering and hearty singing of 'God Bless the Prince of Wales'. When the Royal Party was leaving, the weather had cleared, so the Prince gave orders that his carriage should be opened, so that those who had waited all day could see their Duke and Duchess travelling along the processional route to Trentham Hall with their Royal guests.

During the next two years the building work of Messrs., Tompkinson and Betteley of Longton, progressed on schedule and on October 27th 1899, the, 'Sutherland

Institute, Free Library and Art School' was opened by the Duke of Sutherland accompanied by the American Ambassador. Just prior to the opening of the completed building, the 'Sentinel' described the previous conditions for housing the books which now constituted the new library thus; "The Library has been in the ill-lighted, inconvenient, stuffy upper storey at the centre of the Town Hall building. A room giving the impression that there was an odd space to fill and the library was made to fill it." However, matters were going to be different, from now on!

In the presence of the Magistrates, Members of Council and officials, the Mayor handed His Grace the Gold Presentation Key and requested him to formally open the Institute. It was exactly 3.00 p.m. and once again, everything was on schedule. A short meeting followed, at which the Mayor presided, calling on Alderman Leak J.P., Chairman of the Technical Instructional Committee to make a statement with reference to the Institute. The Duke of Sutherland then addressed the assembly. In conclusion the Mayor made a sincere vote of thanks to His Grace which was seconded by Alderman Ward, Chairman of the Public Libraries Committee.

It was agreed by all that the greatest credit was due to the Longton Corporation for achieving the dignified and imposing ceremony on the visit of H. R. H., the Prince of Wales two years previously and also for the efficiency of the official opening ceremony with the presentation of the Gold Key

Later, the Masonic organising committee said that the visit of the Prince of Wales, "Would be remembered and talked about fifty years hence. The chief actors having crossed, 'The Line of Mystery' but the grandparents of the 1950's would still be living and would be able to tell of making their bow to His Royal Highness in 1897."

I joined the library in 1936, at an earlier age than was strictly legal, after my grandfather persuaded the staff to give me an impromptu reading test. I survived this ordeal and also the very real terrors of the Green, Red and Yellow Fairy Books so thoughtfully provided for children of tender years! I became an 'Adult' member at the age of eleven and the love of books engendered by the library and my family, has continued throughout my life. Today, the Institute is still an elegant and imposing building, which for me, at least, has fulfilled the Prince's wish that it, 'produce fruit one hundredfold.'

PHOTOSTAT: Illustration of the Gold Key

Illustration of Key
(OBVERSE AND REVERSE).

INSCRIPTION.
—

"Presented to
His Grace the Duke of
Sutherland,
on the occasion of the
Opening of the Sutherland
Institute,
October 27th, 1899."

Programme of Ceremony.

HIS GRACE THE DUKE OF SUTHERLAND AND PARTY will be met at the Entrance to the Institute by the Mayor, Magistrates, Members of Council, Officials, &c.

The Mayor will, in the name of the Corporation, hand to His Grace the Presentation Key, and will request him to formally open the Institute.

The Duke will then open the Entrance Door and proceed to the Reception Room on the right of the Main Entrance; the Magistrates, Members of the Council, Officials, &c., proceeding to the adjoining Retiring Room, where they will form in procession to escort the Duke and Party to the Platform.

The Duke and Party will proceed to the Platform, followed by the Magistrates, Members of the Council and Officials, for whom chairs in front of the platform will be reserved.

The Mayor will preside, and will call upon Alderman Leak, J.P. (Chairman of the Technical Instruction Committee), to make a statement with reference to the Institute, after which the Meeting will be addressed by His Grace the Duke of Sutherland, His Excellency the American Ambassador, and Mr. G. W. Smalley.

The Mayor will move a vote of thanks to the Duke.

Alderman Ward (Chairman of the Public Library Committee) will second the vote of thanks.

The Duke of Sutherland will respond.

PHOTOSTAT: Description of the Gold Key

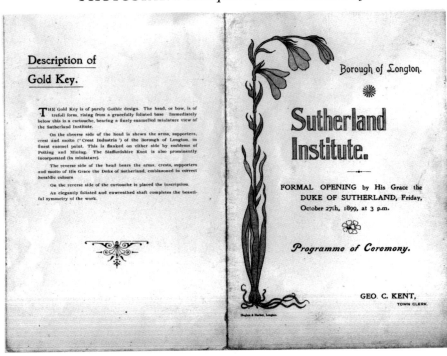

Description of Gold Key.

THE Gold Key is of purely Gothic design. The head, or bow, is of trefoil form, rising from a gracefully foliated base Immediately below this is a cartouche, bearing a finely enamelled miniature view of the Sutherland Institute.

On the obverse side of the head is shewn the arms, supporters, crest and motto ("Creat Industria") of the Borough of Longton, in finest enamel paint. This is flanked on either side by emblems of Potting and Mining. The Staffordshire Knot is also prominently incorporated (in miniature).

The reverse side of the head bears the arms, crests, supporters and motto of His Grace the Duke of Sutherland, emblazoned in correct heraldic colours

On the reverse side of the cartouche is placed the inscription.

An elegantly foliated and enwreathed shaft completes the beautiful symmetry of the work.

Borough of Longton.

Sutherland Institute.

FORMAL OPENING by His Grace the DUKE OF SUTHERLAND, Friday, October 27th, 1899, at 3 p.m.

Programme of Ceremony.

GEO. C. KENT,
TOWN CLERK.

The Sutherland Institute 1998

David Freeman

In this rapidly changing world, I was pleased to notice on a recent visit, that some things remain constant at the Library. The smell of polish seemed to be identical to that used in the 1930's, while the entrance doors appear to have their original brass handles, their rich glow revealing generations of tender loving care! Now my grandfather and his friends, in the words of the Masonic Brethren, have crossed, 'The Line of Mystery' many years ago, but I hope in some way, they will ensure that Longton's, 'Temple of Learning' will be there for the children and adults of the twenty first century.

David Freeman

Terracotta bas-relief above the central portico

THE PURSUITS OF POLITICS,

ARTS AND SCIENCE

JOHN GORDON WALLIS - POLITICIAN

On his appointment as Lord Mayor of the City of Stoke-on-Trent in 1980, John Wallis said, "I am honoured, but so far, everything is overwhelming after nomination."

Born in Stone in 1931, his family had always been associated with the railway, and John was no exception. He was a junior porter in 1945, receiving the princely sum of £1.70 per week, but by the time he was sixteen he became the youngest Chairman of a Trades Union Branch for the railway on record.

During National Service, he was an R. A. F., wireless operator for two years, part of which was spent in Cyprus. On his return to 'civvie street' he resumed work in the newly nationalised British Rail, which offered low wages but secure employment.

John Wallis might well have continued to be a 'country boy' if he had not met Jean Goodwin, of Longton, in 1951. A year later they were married and unwittingly, John was on his way to a successful life in local politics. On attaining the highest honour which could be given by the people and their councillors, Arthur Cholerton, a former Lord Mayor described John as, "A first class ambassador for Stoke-on-Trent." Worthy praise indeed, but only achieved after years of dedication and service to both local and national politics.

Coming from a rural area, John was appalled by the inheritance of social deprivation and poor living conditions which, in 1952, still existed in some parts of Stoke-on-Trent. Terraced houses sharing toilets were not unusual but the toilets known locally as 'Ducketts', which after a long drop went straight into the sewer, were something horribly new to him. In addition pollution and the ever present industrial smoke and dirt, strengthened his resolve to enter politics to help the people.

"The sincerity, generosity and friendliness of the people in the City, was apparent from my first day in Stoke-on-Trent."

At the beginning of his political career, John stood for Ward 22 on four successive occasions from 1967 to 1970. Although unelected, he increased the vote for Labour each time from 32% to 41.1% in what was considered to be a Conservative 'stronghold.' His first significant success came in 1970 in a bye-election, due to the resignation of Councillor Cyril Price in Ward 23, when John gained

25% of the votes. From this time he was on the first step of a political career which was to span more than forty-eight years of service to the Labour Party, the L. M. S., and British Rail. It was at this time that John Wallis became aware of the need to strengthen the local party so that it could become an effective unit. He asked a number of forward thinking people of similar persuasion to become Labour Party members. One of these was Eric Wilkinson, Headmaster of Normacot Junior School for fourteen years and at this time, Headmaster of Brookhouse Green School. Soon, Eric became Secretary to the Ward and later, stood for the Council and John recalls that "The local party was strengthened by such people at a crucial stage in our development."

Subsequent years saw John Wallis winning the annual local elections of 1971 and the last District and City Elections of 1973, polling 39% of the County vote. New heights were to be reached in 1979 when he won 63% of all votes for Longton South, this success continued, unbroken, until 1993. It is obvious that since 1971 local people had crossed the line of party politics and had given their votes and their trust to the councillor who had shown loyalty and had given service most steadfastly. Even in the, 'far-away realms' of the County Council his hard work was recognised by a 39.8% result in 1981.

Throughout those years, John progressed steadily from the 'back-benches' to occupy positions of increasing responsibility. As can be seen, he served continuously until Local Government re-organisation in 1974 when the powers of the City and County Councils merged and then again until his retirement, due to ill-health, in 1992.

The Lord and Lady Mayoress of Stoke on Trent, 1980

John and Jean Wallis

When appointed Lord Mayor of the City of Stoke-on-Trent in 1980, John Wallis had already been a Labour Party Member for twenty-seven years. Regarded by the electorate and fellow party members as dependable, dedicated and generally holding the, 'middle view,' John was known as an extremely able speaker, who could become forceful and relentless when arguing the case for the lives and interests of local people and also for the City in which he had made his home.

It is worthy of note that during his Mayoral Address, he based his speech on the advisability of a return to Unitary Status for the city as soon as was possible. Such was his regard for Stoke-on-Trent, and its people!

Jean Wallis has supported her husband at every turn of his political career, since 1952. Always a person in her own right, she was an active Trades Union and Labour Party member becoming secretary to the former Ward 22 and then election agent for John. Fundraising and organising social events for the Party became a normal part of her life, inspite of being an accomplished free hand paintress at Aynsley China and later at the Denton Works from 1960 onwards. An active member of C.A.T.U., Jean's additional commitments included serving on the Stoke-on-Trent Social Services Advisory Committee.

Essentially a quiet and modest family man, John Wallis said in 1980 and again when we spoke together in 1998, "I am so proud to have had a Potteries Lady as my wife."

John's original precept that he was resolved to 'enter politics to serve the people' has affected the whole of his political and private life. His numerous chairmanships have included the Social Services Advisory Committee, the City Housing Committee, as well as those of Countryside and Highways and the Vice-Chairmanship of the Education Committee. Wide ranging community involvement resulted in committee work with the Staffordshire Police Authority and the Fire Service. He formed the 'Vietnam Support Group' and was closely involved with the resettlement and subsequent welfare of the refugees.

Always realising that education was the way to the future, his work extended to specific schools and over the years he has been Chairman of the Board of Governors at Sandon and Longton Junior High Schools as well as at Alexandra Middle School, Florence Junior and Infants and The Grange School, Meir.

'High Hopes and Banners for the School Which Never Came.'

John Wallis with Normacot Infants.

Always mindful of the wider field of politics, John acted as election agent for Jack Ashley M.P., on four occasions. Community involvement and a sense of service to others has extended to the lives and careers of his daughters; Susan is a Deputy Headteacher and Deborah is a Senior Social Worker.

Commitment to the Trades Union Movement has never wavered for John Wallis; a member of the N.U.R., for forty-eight years, he became Branch Chairman, representing fellow members at National Conferences. Equally steadfast in his spiritual precepts he served as a member of the Parochial Council at the Church of the Holy Evangelists, Normacot and in 1980 invited the Vicar of Normacot, the Rev., Colin Lantsbery, to act as his Chaplain during his Mayoral year.

When assessing his personal aims and memories, John spoke sincerely about those people he regarded as stalwarts and giants of local politics. "During my early days on the Council, they had no large cars or limousines; transport was a bicycle, motorbike or bus! The people who gave me an insight into the needs of the City were Jim Westwood, Sir Albert Bennett, Tom Beddow, Doris Robinson and Horace Barks."

His clearest memory of his Mayoral year was the Queen's visit to the City. "Her Majesty was well informed and sincerely interested in conditions for the people and particularly of those working in the Pottery Industry. I remember the Queen asking some searching questions when we visited the Doulton Factory!" John Wallis still feels most strongly that he was the Queen's representative in

Stoke-on-Trent and is proud that the title of, 'Lord Mayor,' one of only twenty-six in the country in 1980, was of real importance to the people. He enjoyed his visit to Buckingham Palace and has vivid memories of meeting Princess Diana at the Garden Party.

John Wallis's views on the possibility of an elected Mayor are strongly negative. 'The snag would be the introduction of professionalism and business interests. The Office of Mayor needs impartiality, accessibility and friendship for the electorate. All this would be lost if the American type of Mayor with a concern for the popular vote became the norm in Britain. That is not the way forward.'

In retirement, John is kept busy pursuing his life-long interests in cricket and gardening; the latter being brought to a standard of almost complete self-sufficiency! However, the 'country boy' who has served the City dwellers for nearly half a century retains his Party Membership, and let no-one be mistaken, he still brings matters of importance to the notice of officials. At these times, the skilled and forceful speaker can be heard once again and quite clearly. Often dubbed as, 'A man of the people' he is still decisive and effective in the political arena.

DR FREDERICK ARTHUR CHALLINOR (1856 - 1952)

'NORTH STAFFORDSHIRE'S FORGOTTEN COMPOSER'

Challinor was born in humble circumstances and from early childhood showed remarkable force of character and persistence of effort. He had a strong desire to pursue literary tendencies and strangely, this was coupled with great physical endurance. His father was a coal miner and also a Methodist local preacher. Neither of his parents were noticeably musical.

At the age of ten, Challinor left school and worked in a brickfield where the hours were long and the work exhausting. When he was twelve he worked in the weighing house of a colliery for a while before going underground full-time. At fifteen, his uncle arranged for him to work in the 'slip-house' of a china factory. It was here that Challinor's musical education began! Another boy at the factory had been a member of a local workhouse band and it was during their short breaks together that his first instruction in the rudiments of music started.

Some time later, the family received a legacy, part of which was a cottage piano. This gave the stimulation and interest necessary to build on the little he knew.

Early days in Normacot with his daughter, Mabel.

He studied alone, using 'Gauls Harmony'; he was not successful! Saving what little money he could, he took private lessons in harmony and related subjects when he was twenty-one. From now on, he 'thought' music at all times. Not a moment was wasted; harmony exercises were worked, even while eating his meal at the factory. Stainer's Harmony Primer was 'devoured' in ten weeks, such was his desire for academic attainment.

One year later he took his local Royal Academy of Music examination and in two years he entered the Diploma examination of the Royal College of Music. This required a knowledge of five part harmony, Counter-point (both triple and invertible), Fugue, Canon, Instrumentation and Musical Form. His results were so outstanding, that he was not required to stay in London for the Viva Voce examination on the second day.

Undaunted, and with hardly a pause, his next step was to obtain a Bachelor of Music Degree. Consider the magnitude of his task as he set out for a full day's work at the factory, from his home in Alexandra Road, Normacot.

He met with great difficulties at this stage of his studies. The gaps in his early education were immense and disheartened, he returned to his own work in composition. While still at the factory he began to build a circle of private pupils. Gradually, he was achieving the status of musician in his own community and was greatly encouraged by the immediate interest of publishers in his early works.

In 1895 he gave up his work at the china factory and resumed studies for his Bachelor of Music degree. He entered the March examinations and passed in Arts. In the same week, he passed the first music examination and after sending up his 'exercise' in composition in September he attained high success in his degree, which was awarded in 1897. Now, his creative faculty had free play and he showed renewed enthusiasm for the varied forms of anthem, part-song and cantata. They became popular very quickly and a number were used for competitive work by local choirs.

Originally, choirs were formed to improve the behaviour of the masses, but now largely due to the influence of the Welsh miners living locally, competition and prestige were the order of the day! Also, the churches and chapels were moving away from reading and instruction and now Bible stories, singing and 'Tonic Sol Fah' were taking over.

At all times, Challinor spoke through his music in a language which all could understand. It is no surprise that in 1903, when be became DOCTOR CHALLINOR (Dunelm) that he had already over four hundred of his compositions published.

Only privately would he know how much was implied by this achievement. Acknowledging the many letters of congratulation he received, he said, "This proves that there are kind hearts everywhere, and many of them."

Challinor's musical style was genuinely individual in both words and music. He always worked in accepted forms which were effective and practical; no 'great forces' were needed as his musical directness revealed his highly cultured musicianship. His, 'Sunday School Hymns', revealed sympathy and real understanding of the child mind. The 'Musical Messenger,' of 1905 describes them as, 'Polished little gems.'

Dr. Challinor
Composer 1905 (from a photocopy)

His growth to maturity is shown in his cantatas, with their melodic invention and richer, more varied harmonies. 'Bayley and Ferguson' of London and Glasgow published five of his Sacred Cantatas and three Secular Cantatas. Each of these is highly individual in style. For example; 'Judah in Babylon' for Soprano and Baritone solos with Chorus and Orchestra lasted for 70 minutes and had twelve numbers. The, 'Daily Telegraph,' said "It exhibits life and freshness".

Conversely, 'The Gardens of the Lord' was in four sections, each of which could be performed separately. This composition was performed at the Victoria Hall, Hanley, by the Bethesda Choir, conducted by James Garner, the founder of the Hanley Glee and Madrigal Society, and a musician of distinction.

'Bethany' described the raising of Lazarus and had four soloists and chorus, while 'The Journey of Life' and 'The Story of Jesus' were written for juvenile choirs. They had two and three part choruses and it is interesting to note that the former composition had a Welsh translation to accompany the text. Both of these cantatas are classics in their genre.

Challinor's Secular Cantatas include, 'A Pageant of the Year' with both pro-
logue and epilogue. It was suited to choral societies needing a work occupying
half a programme. The 'Song of the Sea,' according to his publishers was a,
"Musicianly and interesting work". The third Secular Cantata, 'Concordia' dealt
with friendship among the nations of the British Isles, the Commonwealth,
Europe and America, which were represented by appropriate characters in a
pleasant and amusing way, the two part choruses being suitable for young
voices and a degree of pagentry.

Further publications show the scope and variety of Challinor's music, with
Anthems for Harvest, Easter and Anniversaries as well as hymn tunes. To
many people the melody, 'Shirley' sung to the words, 'For the Beauty of the
Earth,' sums up his talent and his ability to reach out to the hearts of the
people. This was sung for the first time at the Hospitals' Festival in Hanley
Park in August 1903.

Another of his hymn tunes, 'Tell me the Stories of Jesus' is number 858 in the
Methodist Hymnal, and was sung to great effect in the television series, 'Songs
of Praise' in recent years.

Composition of part songs feature throughout his life, the finest of which, 'Is
My Lover on the Sea?' was performed by the North Staffordshire Choral Society. Challinor was commissioned frequently to write both large and small
scale works for important occasions in the City of Stoke-on-Trent. His 'Ode to

Beauty' is a fine example of this. He wrote both words and music for the prestigious Historical Pageant celebrating the bi-centenary of Josiah Wedgwood in May 1930. He dedicated this work to his granddaughter, Winifred.

'Tell me the Stories of Jesus'

Original manuscript

However, unaccompanied part-songs showed him at his very best. They are akin to the madrigals of Elizabethan England and bear no resemblance to the 'harmonised' melodies which were so popular in the early years of the twentieth century.

Challinor wrote much poetry as well as being deeply involved with his music; some of it has the touch of genius and was published readily. Certain verses reveal the inner man and on reading one poem, in particular 'Retrospection,' I agree with the views held by his grand-daughter, Mrs Winifred Adams Webb, of Blythe Bridge. Her childhood memories of him are quoted with her permission; they relate to a lecture she gave some years ago.

"As a child, I hardly knew my grandfather. He separated from his wife, who then returned to teaching, when my mother was fifteen. I have always felt that they were temperamentally unsuited. My grandfather lived in Alexandra Road, Normacot before he retired to Paignton, Devon. As always, his main relaxations were reading and walking. I remember that after we visited him in his beautiful bungalow and garden, he sent us boxes of plums and pears which he had grown. This poem suggests to me that inspite of his fame and achievements, he had not found true happiness. I feel that he never ceased to regret having been estranged from his four children."

Retrospection

What varied fancies fill the soul
Of him, who, having reached the goal
Ambition fixed for his attempt,
Looks back, and now surveys the whole!

Who, having climbed the mountain's steep,
Past fateful crags where torrents leap,
Makes pause, and scans his journey's course
Down to the jewelled valleys deep.

Life's eminence at length attained,
The end achieved, the summit gained,
His conquering spirit droops, his heart
Is by the aching silence pained.

The stressful past of hope and fear
Holds all that memory counts most dear:
His lips confess the thought he feels
'O happiness, thou art not here!'

It has been said that Challinor's music belongs to a populace living in hard times; also that he was the champion of a religious folk tradition when writing music for what was the, 'highspot' of the year for both children and parents at the Sunday School Anniversaries. Against all odds, Challinor enjoyed a success which many professionally trained musicians never achieved. It must be remembered that he could have succeeded easily in a literary career if music had not claimed his energies.

He was a good poet, a talented and sensitive musician and a melodist of the highest order. It would be wonderful if the chapels and choral societies he served so well in the past, could, where they still exist, bring about a revival of his music, which spoke so directly to everyone, both young and old. Then, once again, artists and audiences alike, could feel true enrichment in their hearts and minds as did Challinor, and say,

'We are the Music-makers
And we are the dreamers of dreams.'

O'Shaughnessy (1844 - 1881)

JAMES ALFRED LOVATT 1873 - 1952

Artist, Photographer, Tutor

On April 11th 1891, the Staffordshire Courier reported "James Lovatt has some remarkably fine work on view. A design for tiles is very ingeniously worked out, and a drawing for the decoration of a plate is a delicate piece of work. This young student was a successful competitor for Sir Smith Child's prize, and considering he is only seventeen years of age, with careful training, he has a brilliant career before him.'

During his school days Lovatt excelled at drawing and design and as his artistry developed, he owed much to his teacher, Mr. George Wooliscroft Rhead, at Longton School of Art. During his early twenties JAL began teaching at Longton Art School. The Principal, Mr. Leonard Morse, advised him to leave home and to find good lodgings. Life was opening up for JAL; he was meeting people, needing to socialise and had a position to fulfill. His talent was immense, according to Rhead and Morse, but as there was no money for full professional training, College was out of his reach. JAL's professional life therefore revolved round the needs and requirements of the artistic life in Stoke-On-Trent.

He was equally at home in the genres of oil and water colour and in 1929, he painted an outstanding portrait, in oils, of the miner, Jack Elkin. This was to celebrate the twenty-first anniversary of the Workers' Educational Association, in Longton. The head and shoulders portrait shows the strong, intelligent features and steadfast expression of the man who had enrolled in the first tutorial in 1909 and had seen it become the basis for the North Staffordshire W.E.A., as we know it today.

Jack Elkin attended many W.E.A., summer schools at Balliol College, Oxford. He was a, 'legend' in his own time and was well known to the Master of Balliol, A. D. Lindsay, who accepted the portrait by JAL as a gift from the Longton students. It hung in his rooms at Oxford until 1968 when it was returned to the North Staffordshire W.E.A.

This photograph illustrates an early work in stained glass of JAL's tutor, Rhead. It shows a kitchen dresser with plates and jugs in the background and Rhead, in what must have been a characteristic pose. The use of rich, jewel-like colours of crimson and cobalt and the detailed tracery of head and shoulders, is masterly. *(See back cover)*

George Wooliscroft Rhead

Further work in stained glass by JAL was under the direction of Gordon Forsyth, Principal of the Schools of Art in Stoke-on-Trent from 1920 until his retirement in 1945. The first of such work was a memorial window at Stoke Parish Church; Lovatt was the tutor of the art class which executed the design by Forsyth.

Later, St. John's Church, Longton, commissioned an east window, in memory of Prebendary George Oliver, Rector from 1896 - 1921. Again, Forsyth designed the window and painted the faces in each panel. The Longton Art class and parish-

K. Edwards

ioners, under Lovatt's close direction completed the work. It has been a privilege to read Lovatt's diary for this immense artistic project. Detailed plans, and achievements are listed almost daily. From inception, on the 1st February 1923, to the unveiling of the window on the 24th June 1926, his diary shows the care and committment of the true artist - craftsman at his best.

Cartoon for the East Window, St. John's Church, Longton

The demolition of St. John's Church, Longton and its east window, was, in the minds of many people, an act of wanton destruction. There was no apparent care or concern, on anyone's part, to save even a section of the beauty created by JAL, Forsyth and the adult students and parishioners of Longton.

Lovatt

Happily, there is much evidence of Lovatt's work in two windows at Christ Church, Meir Road, Normacot. One is to the memory of J. B. Wood in 1925 and is entitled 'Suffer Little Children To Come Unto Me.' The other window, completed in 1929, to the memory of M. E. Ball, shows a delightful grouping, 'Mary Sat At the Foot of Jesus and Heard His Word.' In these windows the colours and composition are both beautiful, and dramatic, showing his innate feeling for this medium.

JAL at work on the memorial window.
Water colour by his daughter,
Winifred Lovatt.

Throughout his life, he continued with diverse work which included portraits and landscapes in both oil and watercolour, as well as tile and pottery designs, usually linked with much experimental firing.

In 1910, JAL became Art Master at Longton High School. A letter from the Borough of Longton Education Committee of March 10th confirming his appointment ended, "The salary is to be £1 per week for each week, during which you are actually engaged in such work." Obviously, a prophet is not always secure in his own country! Previously, his many years as tutor in the schools of Art in Fenton and Longton had spanned from 1895 to 1913. He was appointed Master in Charge at Longton Art School in 1913 until 1919.

At home in Ludwall Road.
L to R JAL, his son, Charles,
Grandma Tams, Winifred
Lovatt, his daughter, and his
wife Elizabeth Catherine.

Miss Winifred Lovatt remembered, the wonderful circle of friends, from all walks of life who visited them in Ludwall Road, Normacot. They discussed politics, literature, philosophy, often while JAL painted. "As a young girl I hoped that one day, I would be admitted to that circle. In later life, my father became ill with spinal trouble, and when tuberculosis of the spine was diagnosed, he had years of treatment. Inspite of walking with two sticks and being in pain, he was always optimistic and cheerful. He achieved much artistic work even after retirement."

JAL's extensive photographic record of life in Normacot and Longton is impressive. Once again, with the eye of the true artist, he has captured the essence of those early years of the 20th century. Morse and Rhead were correct about his, 'immense talent.' So too, the Staffordshire Courier on that day in 1891, when he was just seventeen years of age and the world could and should have been before him. Another time and another place might well have made success possible for this man of high endeavour and undeniable artistic talent.

WORLD SCIENCE AND THE ASTBURY BROTHERS

WILLIAM THOMAS ASTBURY 1898 - 1961

Doctor of Science, (Cantab) M.A., F. Inst. P., F.R.S.,

W. T. Astbury was a British Physicist, an X-Ray crystallographer and the first person to use the term, 'Molecular Biology'.

The elder son of Mr and Mrs W. E. Astbury of Normacot, he received his education at Normacot C of E School and Longton High School where he became Head Boy. After winning City, State and Open Scholarships he studied at Jesus College, Cambridge. These scholarships made his university study possible in the days when there were few 'safety nets' in either health provision or higher education.

In 1921 he became Demonstrator in Physics at University College, London with the team of Sir Wm Henry Bragg and then Research Assistant at the Faraday Laboratory Royal Institute in 1923.

The study of fibres and textiles and their future development became his chosen scientific path and in due course he was appointed Director of the Textile Physics Laboratory at Leeds University in 1928.

Using photographic techniques which he himself had developed, he extended his research of natural fibres such as wool, hair and horn. He discovered that when fibre was stretched or wet, different properties were exhibited.

As early as 1938 he offered the first hypothetical structure for the key genetic material, DNA.

During these years he gained an international reputation for his pioneering work and was awarded the Lille University Medal (1933) and the prestigious Gold Research Medal of the Worshipful Company of Dyers (1934). The following year he received the Warner Memorial Medal of the Textile Institute.

His publication of 'Fundamentals of Fibre Structure' 1933 as well as a major work, 'Textiles Under the X-Rays' ten years later, established WTA as a leading authority in this area of research.

During the Second World War he served in the R.A.F., Volunteer Reserve as a Flight Lieutenant.

In 1945, Astbury was appointed to the new Chair of Biomolecular Structure at Leeds University and in 1946 was invited to join the Forest Products Research Board. Industrial and research bodies were now aware that fibre research was of prime importance especially with its obvious application to new industries.

Appointments and awards were a regular feature of WTA's career. They included election to the scientific council at Upsala, a Doctor of Science Degree from Strasbourg University, the Sylvanus Thompson Medal of the British Institute of Radiology (1948) and the Brussels University Medal (1949).
During the 1950's awards were made by Europe and America; the International Scientific Relations Medal of the American Society of European Chemists and election as a foreign member of the Swedish Royal Academy of Science (1956).

Today, we realise that DNA is essential to forensic science as well as to genetic engineering in the prevention and erradication of hereditary disease, while the use of modern fibres is vital to industry and to the housewife.

Throughout his life, W. T. Astbury worked to further scientific knowledge and to direct that knowledge 'Molecular Biology' into practical application which in turn would affect the lives of ordinary people.

NORMAN FREDERICK ASTBURY C.B.E., 1906-1987

Doctor of Science (Cantab) M.A., F.I.E.E., F. INST P., F.R.S.A.

The younger brother of W. T. Astbury, he attended Normacot C of E., School and Longton High School.

Like his brother, he became Head Boy and won City, Major, State and Open Scholarships. In addition, he was awarded the Duke of Sutherland's Gold Medal for outstanding examination results. Without this scholastic and monetary success, Norman Astbury would have been unable to take his rightful place at University amongst his academic peers.

At St. John's College, Cambridge, his immense talent and superb application to any problem presented to him resulted in further success. He obtained a 'double first' degree in the Natural Sciences Tripos and achieved the distinction of being both Scholar and Prizeman. He was awarded the prestigious Hutchinson Studentship for Research, but refused this opportunity. Instead he accepted a post at the National Physical Laboratory (1929-1939) where he was engaged in electro-technical research of a high order.

*1st L.
Mr. Wm. (Bill)
Wilkinson.
2nd R.
Miss O. M. Wilkinson
Small Bridesmaid:
The Author*

In 1933 he married Miss Nora Enid Wilkinson of Normacot and their first years together were spent in Teddington.

At the outbreak of war in 1939 he was transferred to H.M., Anti-Submarine Research and Experimental Establishment at Portland, subsequently becoming head of an Admiralty Research Division in Scotland. In 1944 he was appointed Principal Scientific Officer with sole responsibility for all aspects of anti-submarine experimental data.

Throughout these years and for a considerable time after the war, his findings and experiments were 'classified', deemed secret.

Postwar saw NFA in the top ranking of industrial research. As Director of Scientific Research in the laboratories of Joseph Sankey and Sons (1945-1949) and on the formation of the Guest, Keen and Nettlefold Steel Corporation, Norman Astbury took over the entire planning of the new, custom-built Research Centre, for the whole company.

He found all aspects of industrial research both fulfilling and exhilarating but the 'pull' of independent scientific research in academic surroundings was hard to resist.

1949 saw him at the New South Wales University of Technology, where the Foundation Chair of Applied Physics was brought to new heights under his guidance.

Greater research facilities were offered to him at Khartoum University where he was Professor of Physics from 1951 until 1956. Whilst at Khartoum he published extensively on electro-magnetics and electro-acoustics, notably 'Magnetic Testing' 1952 and 'Applied Physics' 1956.

N. F. Astbury
on receiving his Doctorate at
St. John's College, Cambridge.

After spending one year at the Royal Aeronautical Establishment at Farnborough, where once more, much of his work was 'classified', Astbury returned to the Potteries, for what was to be the final stage of his career. This was as Deputy Director of the British Ceramic Research Association (1957) and then as Director of Ceramic Research from 1960 until his retirement in 1973.

As Director, he forged new and vital links between industry, polytechnics and universities. His enthusiasm for research and his quest for scientific knowledge remained unabated throughout his life. His eye for detail and superb organising skills made his years as Director outstanding.

Unlike his brother, Norman Astbury enjoyed two hobbies, model railways and music.

Wherever he lived there was always room set aside for tracks, signals and engines; inevitably his 'play' was intense and highly scientific!

Astbury was an excellent pianist and enjoyed a wide ranging keyboard repertoire but preferred the music of the Baroque period above all others. Reading intricate music at sight was both an enjoyment and a challenge, consequently he was in much demand as an accompanist because his powers of immediate concentration resulted in performances of a high standard.

Musical composition was dear to his heart, especially when linked to a well loved poem. In 1947 he was delighted to hear the choir at Longton High School sing his setting of a poem by Robert Bridges, composed whilst he was still a pupil.

Norman Astbury retired to North Devon with his wife Nora and kept in regular contact with scientific colleagues at the Admiralty and in industry until his death in 1987

'NEITHER A LENDER NOR A BORROWER BE'

The Story of Thomas Clarke Wild (1864-1939)

St. Mary's Works, Uttoxeter Road, Normacot
Businessman, Potter, Philanthropist and Politician

The Wild family settled in North Staffordshire in the late 1700's. Isaac Wild was a surgeon in Hanley; his son, William, lived in Cocknage and was the great, great grandfather of 'T. C. Wild'. He married twice; firstly to Catherine who died childless in 1804 and secondly to Mary Clarke, of Trentham. William became a builder, and had pottery and beer selling interests. By the age of twenty-seven he had established himself as, 'William Wild & Company'.

Mary Clarke Wild had five sons and the third eldest, Isaac, succeeded his father as a potter's thrower. In 1833, Isaac married Fanny, the daughter of James Shelley, of Croxden; they had eight children. Their fourth son, Thomas, born in 1841, was the father of 'T.C.' Wild.

Coming from generations who had shown endeavour and strength of purpose, it is no surprise to find 'T.C.' Wild showing the same traits of character. What is quite amazing, is the way in which he achieved success, the scope of that success, and the care and concern he always showed to those he met, or worked with throughout his life.

As a 'half-timer', he worked as a jigger-turner at Albert Barlow's pottery factory for one shilling per week. The hours were 6.00 a.m. until 1.00 p.m., after which his attendance was required at St. James' Church School, Longton. Even whilst at school, he wanted to augment his wages, so he carried water to local residents from the many pure springs in the Normacot area. After leaving school he became a modeller and mould maker, earning one shilling and sixpence per week. True to 'family' again, he became under manager at Barlows at eighteen and married Emily Trickett, daughter of a Longton butcher when he was twenty-one.

'T.C.'s' career was now on the move. As a 'sideline' he became a confectioner; his wife kept the shop whilst he 'potted'. Later, he bought a fruiterers shop in Longton and soon had two more shops selling fruit and confectionery. In all, his 'Empire' covered Stafford Street, Commerce Street and High Street.

In 1891, he bought a small pottery in Clayton Street, Longton, by which time, his father, Thomas Wild, had bought the Albert Works in Longton; the name commemorated the birth of Prince Albert. 'T. C.' joined his father and 'Thomas Wild & Co.,' was born. He became a true part of Normacot, when be bought the St. Mary's Works, in Uttoxeter Road. In 1906, he had said "One day, I will own that factory," and he did just that.

Nora Wild, his daughter, recalled one of his sayings in her book, 'T. C. Wild, My Father'

"If you think you are beaten you are.
If you think you dare not, you don't.
If you think you would like to win
And think you can't; it's most certain you won't!"

T. C. Wild liked to win! As the years went by, he acquired eleven pottery factories and went into partnership with his brother, James Shelley in 'Wild Bros.,' at the Edensor Crown China Works. He made additions to the St. Mary's works in Normacot, updating machinery and changing the old ways of firing the bottle ovens. He built his own generating plant to achieve the mechanical firing of the ovens using gas and electricity.

The range of bone china ware produced at St. Mary's was extensive, with tableware, tea and breakfast sets, all at competitive prices. When his sons Tom and Fred were old enough to join him in business, he made sure that they knew every stage of production. Fred became the technical manager and Tom was in charge of the sales and commercial side of the trade.

By now, the 'Derby ' Pattern was superior to ware produced by other Longton China manufacturers and when a New Zealander, Mr. John Raine, came to the Potteries, seeking agencies, 'T.C.' was ready. Soon the Royal Albert overseas agency was established, the trade mark accepted and the vast markets of Australia and Canada were ready to receive fine china from Uttoxeter Road. As well as the usual extensive range of products, elegant designs for the more expensive markets were produced successfully.

A great love of orderliness in both business and civic duties was always apparent in T. C.'s life, as was his respect for those who worked for him and with him.

In 1914, he wanted to improve the lives and happiness of the people of Normacot. "They need a picture-house; there is the land. I'll buy it and build them a picture house. The 'Alhambra' did bring happiness and a sense of community to the people, and has a story of its own.

In 1916, 'T.C.' moved to Blythe House at Blythe Bridge, Nora Wild remembers the loving and joyous home with its luxurious, but well earned lifestyle. His second wife in 1915 was Ada Eves of Birmingham, who was a kind and understanding 'mother' to the nine daughters and two sons of the first Mrs. Wild who died in 1914. "We had tennis, clockgolf, large gardens, greenhouses and a kitchen garden, as well as a farm. There was a lovely dining room and a large music room where much entertainment was enjoyed," recalls Nora.

Blythe House.

Blythe Bridge High School occupies this site now.

BLYTHE HOUSE

All the girls wore white dresses and sashes which were clean every day. T. C. was loving, but strict. There were no games on Sundays! Their personal bank accounts were checked each month and were closed if evidence of lending or borrowing was discovered. Initials were even engraved on sewing scissors, brushes and combs so that everyone used their own equipment. His precept of "Neither a lender nor a borrower be", was the cornerstone for both himself and his family.

'T. C.' served the community well; he was Church Warden at Normacot for twenty two years and his generosity extended to the Free Churches as well as to the Church of England. He was manager of the Normacot Church Schools, a member of the Etruscan Lodge and became an Income Tax and Land Tax

Commissioner. He was Chairman of the Longton Cottage Hospital Extension Scheme and £3,300 was subscribed by his companies to the Longton War Memorial Fund. At Federation of the City in 1910, he was elected as a Council Member and held office until 1920, when he became an Alderman. He was the first person to hold the title of Lord Mayor, when the City of Stoke on Trent was established in 1925, with the granting of Letters Patent in 1928, the year of T.C.'s office.

T. C. retired to Rhyl and died there in 1939 keeping his interests and activities to the end. In 1949, the East Window of the Church of the Holy Evangelists, Normacot, was given in his memory by the Wild family. This beautiful window and the St., Mary's Works are fitting memorials to a man who maintained that there was no such word as, 'Can't.'

T. C. Wild

Postscript

19.3.1998   Royal Doulton announced that St. Mary's Works was to close in three years.

10.12.1998   Workers of many years standing were given notice without warning. Everyone, including the Potters Union C.A.T.U., was shocked at the speed and number of proposed redundancies (approx. 100) as well as news that St. Mary's would close as early as June 1999.

According to management, difficulties were due to the strong pound, overstocking of certain ware and long delays for delivery. Workers referred to millions lost in Indonesia and that overseas visitors preferred to buy ware marked 'Made in England'. St. Mary's is a listed building and will remain, but what of the workers? No doubt they will be 'retrained' but generations of skill and knowledge of their unique industry will be lost.

T. C's maxim seems to apply.

"If you think you are beaten, you are"

The Alhambra Cinema - Normacot's 'Moorish Palace'

Built in 1914, by T. C. Wild, the pottery manufacturer, for the people of Normacot, the 'Alhambra' Cinema no longer exists. It was a landmark for eighty years, closing in 1977 and demolished in 1994 to make way for the new A50 and the aptly named, 'Alhambra Roundabout'.

The 'Alhambra' had the distinction of being one of the earliest purpose built cinemas in the country, with its unique frontage standing out most handsomely, from the rows of terraced houses, small shops and fish and chip, 'emporia' which clustered around it. In the early days, many cinemas were adapted to show the new silent films; not so the 'Alhambra'. No theatre pillars or boxes obstructed one's view, and although the films were relatively short, the fact that they were projected directly on to a screen enhanced their quality. Elsewhere, many films were shown on unsteady, make-shift structures, which resulted in the type of images giving rise to the term, 'A night at the flicks!'

Originally, singers, dancers and variety acts performed between the films; at the 'Alhambra' they were ably accompanied by Arthur Coleman's small orchestra, with Bill Harvey as drummer and Basil Dobson, principal violin. They made the drama of the silent films come alive for the unsophisticated audiences of those early days. The standard of performance was high, as most of the musicians were employed professionally by the local variety theatres.

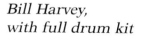

Bill Harvey,
with full drum kit

Bentley

Silent films in a purpose built cinema laid a firm foundation for future generations of attendance; Chaplin, Keaton and Mary Pickford were viewed with ease in gracious surroundings. The managers, and later co-owners from 1945 onwards were Levison Myatt and his brother, Arthur. They gave continuity of service for over fifty years, maintaining the highest standards during that time. With the Myatts at the, helm, once we had taken our seats, the world of Normacot faded quickly as the 'Silver Screen', heightened our imagination and reality was suspended for a few glorious hours! Our cinema saw us through the decades, when only too late, we realised that the world and its values had changed beyond repair. So, why bother to remember? Why try to recapture the memory of 'glamour' and excitement straight from Hollywood? The answer is simple; the story of the, 'Alhambra' is not just our story in Normacot, but that of the cinema industry, its devotees and its development throughout Britain.

My first memories of the, 'Alhambra' were during the late 1930's. Born in Torquay, my small world had been encompassed by sand, sea, infants school and music on the promenade, none, of which had prepared me for my initial experience of a Saturday Matinee.

I remember walking up the few steps to the double glass doors, knowing that Grandpa Wilkinson was excited because his favourite star, Tessie O'Shea, was in the main picture. One of the doors was opened promptly by the Commissionaire, Mr. Broad, magnificent in his full regalia of crimson, gold braid, military cap and white gloves. He saluted grandpa and bowed slightly to me.

The Manager, Levison Myatt was on duty in the foyer, dressed in his 'working' clothes which were a black jacket and trousers, white dress shirt and black bow tie. I was introduced to him and was then allowed to buy the, 'tickets' which were made of aluminium. Later, I discovered that their different shapes of squares and circles were used to assess the size of the audience. Then, with the tension associated with the unfamiliar, the unknown, as well as the unreal, I walked upstairs to the circle, passing mural panels of pastoral scenes in delicate colours. At the top of the stairs, I saw the waiting room with its red plush seating and then quite suddenly, I was steered through red velvet curtains and entered this, 'other world.'

The lights were on, so we chose our own seats. Looking round I saw the shiny silk curtains covering the screen and was amazed at the ornate ceiling and coloured plasterwork over the proscenium arch. Music played softly through the loud speakers, as the days of Coleman's Orchestra were long gone and the, 'Alhambra' never had an organ installed.

As I settled in my seat there was great activity in the stalls below with constant talking, some shouting and a great deal of running about. Soon, a gentle, but easily identifiable smell of other peoples oranges rose to balcony level. Order was restored, to a degree, by the usherette, who walked along each aisle with a cane. Children were quiet as she went by and then chaos broke out again behind her. Later, at school, I learned that Saturday mornings were far worse when the 'Two-penny Rush' occurred. Mrs. Stonier, the usherette, shouted, 'Two in a seat' at the small boys who she always viewed with suspicion, often searching under seats for them when programmes changed. At Christmas, Levison Myatt, who had no children of his own, always made sure that each child had a present of an orange and some sweets.

Suddenly, the lights dimmed, the curtains parted to the accompaniment of whistles, cheers and clapping from the stalls below. The show had started! First there was a cartoon, followed by the Pathe News. Just before the main feature began I was aware that the Commissionaire was spraying a fine perfumed mist high over our heads. Afterwards, he leaned over the balcony, took aim, sprayed with some determination and then left, quietly, his hygiene duties completed! Grandpa and I enjoyed the main film immensely and then there was an interval before the second film was shown. 'Eldorado' ices were for sale; Levison Myatt refused to sell sweets and chocolate at the cinema because of the difficulties faced by the local shopkeepers during the 1930's. In the balcony, the 'select few' were offered the alternative of a cup of tea and a biscuit during the matinee interval; china cups from T. C. Wild of course!

When I arrived at school on Monday morning, two boys were re-enacting fights and scenes from the films to a large and attentive crowd under the iron-staircase. This performance was for those who could not afford to attend the cinema twice a week and would therefore, miss out on details in any serial films. Economic necessity being what it was, a small fee or a good 'swop' was expected from the onlookers.

It is impossible for anyone born after 1970 to realise the impact of the cinema on ordinary people. It was the, 'Great Educator' for at least three decades, showing us how to walk, talk, dress and behave. Ladies fashions and hairstyles were copied slavishly by many, even if they were somewhat passee when they arrived in Normacot. For the T.V., addicts of the 1990's an advertisement in the Church Magazine brings matters into focus. "If your friends are not at home, you'll find them at the, 'Alhambra'.

Lovatt

The Commissionaire in full regalia.
Films showing: 'Escape of Jim Dolan' and, 'Black Spot.'

During the war, shift workers, men on leave, women and children inched their way forward in the queue hoping for a seat or even standing room. The fish and chips shops did a roaring trade, but chocolate and sweets needed coupons. Enterprising small boys had worked out a 'system' on the Beechnut Chewing Gum machine outside Wain's shop. Every fourth packet was free and having marked the serrated dial they were able to supply the queue at a reasonable price!

Soon news reels began to rival the newspapers; they were up to date and often unbiased. However, as the war progressed, censorship and propaganda prevailed. Slogans on vital national security such as, 'Walls Have Ears,' with a Ministry sketch to follow, how to save fuel and suitable healthy recipes all appeared on screen. The 'Educator' was changing through necessity. National pride and morale was boosted when historical battles were presented. Flora Robson, as Queen Elizabeth I in, 'Fire Over England' saying, "The earth belongs to all men. A navy foremost in the world, not only now, but for generations to come!" We felt neither alone nor intimidated although our convoys were at risk and London was ablaze.

Walking home in the blackout, we had nothing to fear. All the violence was on the screen and even that was minimal; the Hollywood 'tough guy', Humphrey Bogart, rarely hit anyone more than half a dozen times in an entire film.

The postwar years brought many further shortages and again, the, 'Alhambra' helped us to cope with a re-issue of Clarke Gable in, 'Gone With the Wind,' then Bing Crosby, Bob Hope and the beautiful Dorothy Lamour in her exotic sarong! 'The Road to Utopia' and all their other roads were our roads too!

In the early 1960's, cinema audiences began to dwindle and as multi-screen entertainment became the fashion, smaller cinemas survived as, 'Bingo Halls', slipping gradually into decrepit shadows of their former selves. During this decade, almost every home possessed a television set; this did not help cinema attendances. In the case of the 'Alhambra' the dubious delights of the American, 'teen-age myth', in the form of, 'Rock Around The Clock,' with Bill Haley and His Comets helped to hasten its closure in 1977. The Myatt brothers decided that they were not prepared to have this type of entertainment foisted on them by Hollywood, Pinewood Studios, or anyone else.

When the 'Alhambra' was demolished in 1994, its unique facade was saved by one person, Angie Dickinson, of the Heritage Group. After fighting a lone battle to save the cinema, and showing unstinting moral courage over many months, on the day of demolition she showed great physical courage, when she demanded that at least the facade should be saved. After some 'debate', with Angie esconced on the roof of the building, the construction company for the A50 roadworks, agreed to have each brick numbered for future identification, this at their own expense. Angie is now the owner of the dismantled facade and has strong feelings about its future.

The Author

'Standing Alone'

If the 'Alhambra' does rise, Phoenix-like from the ashes, it should be as a working cinema, in Normacot, or nearby. Many people feel that a future existence as a facade in a museum setting, would be a costly and meaningless exercise.

The tourist quarter is not far away, with the Gladstone Pottery, factory shops and the Wedgwood Visitor Centre at Barlaston attracting American, Japanese and European visitors. A custom built, 'art-deco' cinema showing specialist films, could well succeed as a commercial venture with initial help from the private and public sectors. It might even serve the people of Normacot once again, if the same high standards of T. C. Wild and the Myatt brothers were reached. How wonderful it would be if, in the twenty-first century, the old advertisement of the 1940's were true, once more . . .

"If your friends are not at home,
you'll find them at the Alhambra!"

'NORMACOT'S DOCTORS'

Dr. Edward Joseph Heslin (1900 - 1957)

Dr. 'Jim' Heslin was born in the West of Ireland and trained at the University of Galway. His first appointment was at the Martyr Hospital, Dublin and it was here that he developed his special interest and skill in midwifery.

In 1924, he wanted to, 'See The World,' so he joined the Alfred Holt, Blue Funnel Line of Liverpool. At first, he was ship's doctor for short hauls, but after proving his competence, he really did expand his horizons with long voyages to the Far East. After a few years at sea, he became assistant to Dr. Lloyd Griffiths, of Wrexham. Being a true Celt, he not only learned Welsh, but became quite proficient in the language.

Circa 1930, he came to Normacot to join the practice of the well respected Dr. Burgess, of Chaplin House Surgery. He took charge of the practice on the death of Dr. Burgess, and in1933, Dr. Heslin married Florence (Betty) Wild, a niece of the famous T. C. Wild. They had two children, John and Elizabeth.

During the second World War, his duties were heavy. He took responsibility for the patients of doctors serving in the armed forces and his daily routine consisted of morning surgery at Chaplin House followed by one at the Meir. These duties were repeated in the evening, while house visits had to be fitted in after lunch and evening surgery. Dr. Heslin found it difficult to drive in the war time, 'Black-out,' so his wife drove the car for evening house visits. His son, now Monsignor John Heslin, of St. Patrick's R. C., Church, Stafford remembers that the old dark red Citroen OVT 555, 'Seemed to go on for-ever!'

He also recalls, "The cellar was out of bounds to me, because the medicines were kept there in a perfectly constant temperature. Also, I remember that during the war, the entrance hall was blocked off to form a shelter for the family, as well as for neighbours and any patients who might have been attending surgery."

Dr. Heslin was tall and dark, with a strong outgoing personality allied to a fiery temper when meeting foolishness or injustice. Older residents, however, remember that his kindness and compassion to patients was of the highest order. His care of those suffering from cancer was untiring. Some still call him, 'Mr. Normacot.' "Heslin had a great ability to diagnose and his treatments were often immediate," recalled Harry Dawson. "One day my mother's knees had filled with fluid; orders were given for a kaolin poultice to be prepared, cotton pyjamas torn into strips and the poultice applied. It was quick and effective relief to a woman who had been screaming with pain."

In 1945, Dr. Ann Hoey M.B, B.Ch., BAO., became Dr. Heslin's assistant. She trained at Dublin University College of the National University of Ireland, qualifying in 1944. After a year's post graduate studies at the 'Rotunda' Hospital, Dublin, she came to Normacot. With her red hair, youth and vitality, 'Dr. Anne' became immensely popular with her patients. Her expertise, kindness and her genuine interest, not only in the patient, but in the family as a whole, is still remembered and appreciated.

Dr. Heslin's life was not destined to be a long one. In 1957, cancer of the oesophagus was diagnosed. He attended the John Radcliffe Hospital for his operation and subsequent treatment. "He returned home and had a bedroom downstairs," said his son. "Dr. Hoey was a good friend to him at this time, but inspite of much care, he lost his vitality; the old fire had gone." Dr. Heslin remained at Chaplin House until his death in December 1957.

The view down Chaplin Road. Circa 1910.
No trees, litter or vehicles.

Chaplin House still serves the people of Normacot, but in quite a different way; it is now a mosque. This centre of worship, community and culture has an extended facade which incorporates the original house. It is delightful to see the children arriving for instruction, carrying their copies of the Koran. All are beautifully dressed and well behaved, at least on these occasions!

Monsignor Heslin has visited his old home since it became a mosque and was impressed by the alterations, as well as the courtesy shown to him by the Imam. However, he said, "Inspite of our Catholic faith and the fact that I trained for the priesthood, none of us realised that our front door faced East!"

Doris Maude Evelyne Carrington M.B. Ch.B.,

Born at the turn of the century in Sutton Coldfield, Dr. Doris Carrington was the elder of two daughters of a Chartered Accountant. She began her training at Birmingham University at the end of the First World War when she found that her fellow students were mainly men returning from the battlefields to resume or begin their studies. Their experiences in the war had a profound effect on her and instilled a sense of duty and compassion from which all her patients benefitted for over forty years.

On graduating, she became assistant to Dr. Hawley whose main practice was in Blythe Bridge, but who also had a surgery in Normacot, It was this surgery, in Uttoxeter Road, which Dr. Carrington took over on her own, and where she lived and worked until her retirement.

Surprisingly, for a woman in the 1920's and 30's, she was a keen and knowledgeable follower of sport, holding a Stoke City season ticket for many years. Male patients were often surprised to receive a detailed analysis of the team's fortunes along with the medical advice they had sought! Dr. Carrington was a participant as well as a spectator, playing tennis at the Blythe Bridge courts and golf at the old nine hole course at the Meir.

After retiring in the mid 1960's, she lived at Rough Close with her husband, Norman Wardle, a Director of the Star and Garter Road sand and gravel company. She pre-deceased him in 1971 after a short illness, but the memory of her kind and gentle personality will always be treasured by both her friends and former patients.

CARE IN THE COMMUNITY

LONGTON COTTAGE HOSPITAL 1868 - . . . .

Lovatt

Longton Cottage Hospital Matron Miss S. E. Barton and Nurses. 1907

LONGTON COTTAGE HOSPITAL.

LONGTON COTTAGE HOSPITAL.
Founded by John Aynsley on land given by the Duke of Sutherland.
Postmarked 1910.

From a Photocopy

BOROUGH OF LONGTON.

MEMBERS OF THE CORPORATION & PUBLIC OFFICERS.

MAYOR, MATTHEW WARDHAUGH Esq.

ST. JOHN'S WARD. *Aldermen*—G. Copestake, A. Edwards. *Councillors*—D. Chapman, E. F. Coghlan, G. Hallam, J. L. Johnson, A. G. Prince, J. Ward.

ST. JAMES'S WARD. *Aldermen*—J. Hulse, M. Wardhaugh. *Councillors*—W. Cooper, H. M. Williamson, G. E. Farmer, J. Holdcroft, C. Clarke, W. Tomlinson.

ST. PAUL'S WARD. *Aldermen*—J. G. Bakewell, R. H. Hawley. *Councillors*—G. Bennion, A. Colclough, W. Garner, J. Finney, G. C. Kent, R. Wild.

DRESDEN WARD. *Alderman*—J. Chew. *Councillors*—E. Brookfield, W. J. Taylor, T. Hawley.

FLORENCE WARD. *Aldermen*—B. Prowse, J. Leak, J. Ferneyhough. *Councillors*—W. Hudson, W. Lowe, C. Bromley, W. Skelson, T. Freeman, J. Wilson, H. Furber, R. Cooper, J. B. Shelley.

TOWN CLERK—Geo. H. Hawley, Esq.; office, Court House; residence, Blythe Bridge.
BOROUGH SURVEYOR—Mr. J. Wardle; office, Court House.
BOROUGH ACCOUNTANT—Mr. Joseph Shenton; office and residence, Cemetery Lodge.
BOROUGH TREASURER—H. C. Ramsdale, Esq., Bank House, Longton.
BOROUGH AUDITOR—Mr. E. J. Hammersley, Pall Mall, Hanley.
BOROUGH MAGISTRATES—John H. Goddard, Esq., Longton Hall; Joseph Hulse, Esq., Dresden; William Webberley, Esq., Meir House; Thomas Waterhouse Barlow, Esq., Stone; A. Edwards, Esq., Dresden; G. Copestake, Esq., Dresden; R. H. Hawley, Esq., The Foley.
CEMETERY REGISTRAR—Mr. Joseph Shenton, Cemetery Lodge.
CLERK TO BOROUGH MAGISTRATES—Geo. H. Hawley, Esq., office, Court House.
CLERK TO SCHOOL BOARD—G. C. Kent, Esq.; office, Chancery Lane; residence, Dresden.
COUNTY MAGISTRATES—John H. Goddard, Esq., Longton Hall; James F. Wileman, Esq., Oulton, near Stone; J. St. Vincent Parker Jervis, Esq., Parkhall, Longton.
COLLECTORS OF BOROUGH { Mr. T. Harber, for the Longton Rating District.
AND DISTRICT RATES { Mr. H. Malbon, for Florence and Dresden.
COLLECTOR OF ASSESSED TAXES—Mr. J. W. Bromley, office, Vauxhall Street.
COLLECTOR OF POOR RATES—Mr. John Webberley, office, Market Terrace.
COLLECTOR OF GAS ACCOUNTS—Mr. Platt, office, Gas Works.
CORONER—John Booth, Esq., Shelton.
INSPECTOR OF WEIGHTS AND MEASURES—Captain Knight, Stafford.
INLAND REVENUE OFFICER—Mr. Llewellyn, 117, Cobden Street, Dresden.
MANAGER OF GAS WORKS—Mr. J. M. Darwin, offices, Gas Works; residence, Dresden.
MEDICAL OFFICER—W. J. Dawes, Esq., Trentham Road.
REGISTRAR OF BIRTHS AND DEATHS—Mr. G. E. Farmer, 11, Commerce Street.
RELIEVING OFFICER—Mr. T. Marshall, office, Market Terrace.
SANITARY INSPECTOR—Mr. Cooke, Vale Street, Stone Road; office, Court House.
SCHOOL BOARD OFFICER—Mr. Leonard Austin, Orchard Place.
STAMP DISTRIBUTOR—Mr. S. Bullock, Market Street.
STIPENDIARY MAGISTRATE—C. H. Greenwood, Esq., Market Drayton.
SUPERINTENDENT OF FIRE BRIGADE—Mr. Cooke, Vale Street, Stone Road.
SUPERINTENDENT OF POLICE—Mr. McWilliams, Commerce Street.
SUPERINTENDENT OF BATHS—Mr. W. Suchons, the Baths.
SUPERVISOR OF INLAND REVENUE—Mr. Walter, High Street, Hanley.
SURROGATE—Rev. A. Clarke, The Rectory; Rev. J. Finch Smith, Edensor.
TOWN CRIER—Mr. Samuel Harvey, Market Lane.

---

grave that was unhonoured and unsung. Even among the Jews themselves, before Christ came to earth, the poor and the sick had no better fate than that described by our Lord in His parables as a type of their condition. No man gave unto the poor prodigal, and he ate and filled himself with the husks that the swine did eat, and the sick Lazarus lay at the rich man's gate, ate of the crumbs that fell from his table, and only the dogs came to lick his sores.

Now, in our town, in this instance most surely we may assert that our citizenship is of heaven. What is our daily experience? As I go daily to the wards of our hospital, in our Christian town, what do I daily see? What value do our citizens place on human life? There is a rush and hurry in the street, and a child is lifted from the stones where it has been dashed, torn and broken and bleeding, by some hurriedly-passing wheel or startled horse, and within a few minutes women's gentle hands have stripped off the blood-stained clothes, straightened the tortured bones, and grateful insensibility to pain lulls the sufferer to rest, while the surgeon skilfully and swiftly uses the knife, or replaces the dislocated limbs. A dull sound of falling earth is heard in a mine, or a sudden flash tells of an explosion, and soon there is borne to the pit's mouth, and then carried carefully and safely in the ambulance, that charity has provided, something that hardly looks human, blackened, and burnt, a victim to the stern accidents of modern industry, one of the martyrs of toil. Within an hour everything that surgical science and trained nurses' ready-willingness can do, has quieted the writhing body, soothed the restless nerves, dressed the scorched and scathed trunk; while hardly a sigh or a moan does the patient utter, as he bravely bears the pain that even Christian charity can at first only relieve and lessen. From the streets, from the mines, from the factories, from every place where are human beings, and where accidents can happen, are brought such cases, as those I briefly mention, into the wards of the hospital, which you, citizens of Longton, taught of heaven, have now for many years provided.

I again commend its support to you to-day. Nor do I know a better time and place for you to show that charity which is twice blessed, blessing him who gives and him who takes, than after prayer and praise in the House of your Father in Heaven, who "forgiveth all your sins and healeth all your infirmities."

Extract of Sermon preached by the Rev. Adam Clarke, Rector of Longton, on the occasion of the Mayor and Corporation of Longton attending Divine Service in St. James' Church. November 16th 1884.
Text: Philippians 3, 20 "Our conversation (i.e. citizenship), is in Heaven".

LONGTON COTTAGE HOSPITAL

When the Reverend Adam Clarke became the incumbent of St. James, The Less, Longton, no-one could have foreseen the changes he would bring to the parish and its people. He received the living of St. James in 1863 from his mother, who was the patron; hardly an auspicious start for a career of merit!

The environment he encountered was appalling. Substandard houses, gross overcrowding, shared sanitation in the notorious 'courts', gave the impression of a human rabbit warren. Over all this squalor was the constant pall of smoke and soot which pervaded every aspect of daily life. Adam Clarke set to work immediately. By 1864, he had established an, 'Invalids' Kitchen', and dispensary. This was with the help of George Farmer, printer, stationer and Mayor of Longton.

Next, he employed Nurse Field to visit the sick and assess their needs. Often mothers and their children were ill at the same time and the provision of cooked food, bed linen and skilled medical help, must have seemed miraculous. Nurse Field's work continued uninterrupted as her salary and all the costs incurred were paid by the Rector's wife, initially and later by public subscription.

By July 1868, a Cottage Hospital was opened at Mount Pleasant, on ground which was elevated well above the slums of Longton. Today, it would have been in Lawley Street, adjacent to the 'Shire Ceramic' works.

Illustration: The Original Cottage Hospital 1870

Again, the benefactor was the Rev. Adam Clarke. He owned the land and the building and gave them to the townspeople in 1872. He also created a Board of Trustees consisting of eminent citizens and leading manufacturers, one of whom was Wm. Webberley, Chief Bailiff of Longton and a Church Warden of St. James Church.

The total cost of setting up the hospital was £700, the workers contributing £130 of the total sum. Patients made small weekly payments, before and during any care they received. In this way they knew that they were supporting the present and the future of amenities offered and thereby safeguarding the first hospital for local people. They had immediate access to medical care and the long and often terrifying journey to the Infirmary, by whatever means they could muster, would not happen again.

Inspite of this endeavour, infectious diseases became rife due to a rapidly expanding workforce, poor working conditions and inadequate sanitation, as well as the ever present cess pools which bred serious infection. Vaccination was viewed with suspicion by all classes, inspite of the fact that in 1871 there were fourteen deaths from small-pox in one month. Infant mortality averaged 44.4 per thousand that year.

The ground-floor accommodation at Adam Clarke's hospital consisted of two wards, each of four beds, for male and female patients, a surgery, bathrooms and an ice-house. On the first floor there were eleven bedrooms and further small rooms beneath the gables. When Nurse Field became ill through overwork, patients received their special care from Nurse Short, while a 'reliable housekeeper' saw to the daily administration and overall costs. After further successful fund raising, more nurses were employed and later, opportunity for convalescence became possible in the clean air of Alton. This was due to the generosity of a Miss Jackson, who often helped with the care of patients at her farmhouse at Farley.

The goodwill shown by the workers, manufacturers and the medical profession, led by Dr. Arlidge, the consultant physician, was a tribute to the real Christian virtues of Adam Clarke. In 1879, the hospital moved to a new building on the north side of the same street, this having better facilities.

The Cottage Hospital carried on its work for fifteen years. Donations from Wm. Webberley and great generosity from Sir Smith Child, M.P., helped standards to be maintained. The year before his death in 1886, the Rev., Adam Clarke appointed seven new trustees, ensuring that the work of the Board was secure and established.

By this time the Lawley Street site could no longer offer even relatively clean air to its patients. Again workers, manufacturers and trustees came to the rescue. In 1887 a two day 'Christmas Sale,' at Longton Market Hall raised £1,130, in the hope that a new site and new building could be found for the hospital.

Almost immediately, a new site was offered by the Duke of Sutherland, whose patronage was unstinting in every aspect of local life. It was ideal; away from the town's pollution on elevated ground in Belgrave Road, Normacot, near to the Church of the Holy Evangelists.

A new era had begun.

THE MASONIC FOUNDATION STONE CEREMONY

On June 27th 1889 two hundred Masonic Brethren processed from the Wesleyan Chapel to the hospital site in Belgrave Road, the 'Volume of Sacred Law" being carried in their midst.

The Mayor, Alderman John Aynsley, J.P., asked the Rector, Reverend G. F. Tamplin, to announce the first hymn, 'O God, our Help in Ages Past" which was then sung by the whole assembly. Afterwards, a silver trowel with a carved ivory handle, was handed by the Lord Mayor to Mr. George Arthur Prince, Chairman of the Board of Directors. The Chairman adjusted the memorial stone and proved it true, using a plumb-rule and mallet, according to Masonic rites. The plumb-rule and mallet were made of the finest polished mahogany, and were presented to the hospital later, together with the silver trowel.

Many heartfelt references were then made to the late Rector, Adam Clarke, and of the noble part he had played in establishing care for sick and needy people.

Dr. W. J. Dawes, Medical Officer of Health, laid the second memorial stone and said that he had asked the late Rector to ensure the funds necessary for building and promised him that the, 'Medical men were ready and willing to do their part."

William Webberley was presented with the trowel; he laid the third foundation stone and found it true. Initially, he had been reluctant to take part in the ceremony having withdrawn from public life for some time. However, after seeing the endeavours of so many to achieve the new hospital, he felt that he could not stand back. After an excellent address, he hoped that the hospital would, 'Prove a blessing to all the inhabitants of Longton for many years to come."

The fourth memorial stone was laid by His Worship, The Mayor of Longton, Alderman John Aynsley, J.P. Knowing that the work would soon be completed, he added, "I hope that the moneyed gentlemen of the district will open their hearts and their purses, so that the noble work can be fully carried out!" He then presented the guest of honour, Sir Smith Child, with the trowel, saying "The whole county has reason to be proud that they have such a man as you amongst them; a man who is now beyond his eighty-first birthday, and we trust that we shall all live to see you attain your hundredth birthday." The foundation stone is placed at the North East corner of the central building.

The inscription reads:

THIS CORNER STONE
WAS LAID BY
SIR SMITH CHILD, BART.,
AND TRIED AND PROVED BY
COL. FOSTER GOUGH, LL.D.,
THE R.W.P.G. MASTER MASON OF STAFFORDSHIRE,
JUNE 27th, 1889.
THIS STONE CONTAINS COINS AND PAPERS.

Sir Smith Child concluded an eloquent address by saying that those who had assisted in this work, "Were to be found in the cottage as well as in the mansion."

The ceremony continued with the placing of a glass bottle in the prepared stone cavity by Colonel Foster Gough, the newly appointed Right Worshipful Provincial Grand Master for Staffordshire. The bottle contained the latest issues of, "The Longton County Times and Echo, The Staffordshire Advertiser, Staffordshire Sentinel and The Staffordshire Knot". Also included were two of the latest Hospital Reports, one containing the deed of settlement and a list of original trustees.

A glass jar containing coins was placed in another cavity; these were a sovereign for 1889, a half sovereign for 1887, a four shilling piece, a half-crown, florin, shilling, six-pence, a silver threepenny piece, a penny, half-penny and farthing again for 1889.

The Provincial Grand Master, Lt., Colonel Bindley, then gave the plans to the builder, with twenty new shillings to purchase refreshments as a reward to the workmen, for their labours that day. Fifty pounds was placed on the Foundation Stone on behalf of the Masons. Brother G. C. Kent, Hon., Secretary of the Longton Cottage Hospital Committee, placed a cheque for £1,130, which were the proceeds of the Christmas Fair and Sale. This cheque was specially prepared by Hughes and Harber, printers and stationers and was later framed and hung in the new hospital.

According to Masonic tradition, corn was scattered on the Foundation Stone to signify plenty, wine was poured over it for joy and gladness, followed by oil as an emblem of peace.

Mrs Aynsley then received monetary contributions from the factory and colliery workers in the town; these amounted to £512 - 4 - $8^1/_2$ and were contained in one hundred and fourteen purses, carried in procession, by children of the workers. The singing of, 'All people that on earth do dwell," followed by the National Anthem, ended the ceremony.

The Masonic Brethren, then took dinner at Longton Town Hall, and continuing in their generosity, donated a further ten pounds to the Hospital and one guinea towards the Sunday School Annual Treat.

Lovatt

THE NEW LONGTON COTTAGE HOSPITAL
Opened by Mrs Adam Clarke, widow of the Rector of St. James, Longton
on September 25th 1890.

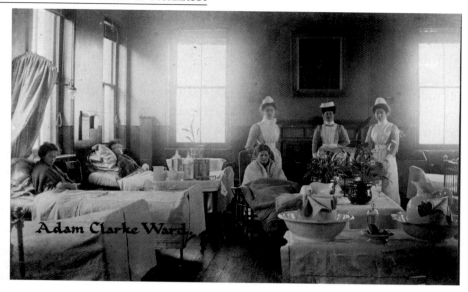

Lovatt

The New Adam Clarke Ward

"A BEACON ON THE HILL'

The building work went ahead with both speed and efficiency due to the expertise of the architects Messrs. Ford and Slater, of Burslem and the contractors, Messrs. H and R Inskip, of Longton. The construction was of brick and terracotta; outward ornamentation was minimal, on the express wishes of the Trustees, who deemed comfort and usefulness to be their priority. The fabric cost £3,359 and when the furniture and appliances were installed, the total cost rose to £6,000. It is worthy of note that all monies were raised by public subscription; more than half being given by the colliery and pottery workers in the area.

The Opening Ceremony September 25th 1890

The opening ceremony commenced at two. A procession was formed at Normacot Church schools, and proceeded to the hospital, headed by Supt. Evans (mounted), the Longton Borough Prize Band, amongst those following being the Bishop of Shrewsbury and clergy, the Mayor and ex-Mayor, magistrates, aldermen, councillors, trustees and directors of the hospital, and others, the Dresden Military Band bringing up the rear. On arrival at the hospital the Longton Choral Society sang the "Hallelujah Chorus," accompanied by the Dresden Band. A very large gathering had assembled in front of the hospital, including Mrs. Adam Clarke, Sir Smith Child, Capt. Edwards - Heathcote, M.P., the Bishop of Shrewsbury, the Mayor of Longton (Alderman J. Aynsley), the Mayor of Stoke (Alderman W. Boulton), Lady Stamer, Lady Buller, Miss Child, Miss Royds, the Rev. H. C. Turner, the Rev. G. F. Tamplin, the Rev. T. P. Forth, the Rev. S. Salt, the Rev. J. Willcock, the Rev. J. Burr Vincent, Messrs. W. Webberley, W. A. Adderley, J. Gimson, J. Hulse, H. Hill, A. G. Prince, W. J. Dawes, T. Forester, J. Dimmock, J. Chew, G. Hallam, A. Edwards, S. Herbert Cooper, H. C. Lynam, G. Bennion, G. H. Frewer, W. R. Blair, T. Blair, Edmund Tearle, H. M. Williamson, J. Leak, Dr. Arlidge, Councillors J. G. Aynsley, R. Cooper, E. Brookfield, W. Skelson, G. E. Farmer, J. L. Johnson, Jonathan Johnson, J. Ward, A. Colclough, E. H. Bloor, T. H. Griffiths, J. Amison, T. Bates, G. Greaves, Chief-Supt. Hill, Drs. A. Parkes, J. W. Jones, A. Averill, Messrs. S. Emony, R. Kent, J. W. Bromley, T. Copestake, T. Heath, Fred. Aynsley, F. Williamson, &c.—Mr. W. R. BLAIR,

Provision was made for thirty-eight beds in three general wards; each had good ventilation, lighting and warmth. The administration block was in the centre of the hospital. The ground floor comprised a board-room, matron's sitting room, two rooms for a commissionaire, a nurses' dining room, nurses' and matron's bedrooms, a kitchen and stores. On the upper floor was a sitting room for the nurses and further bedrooms. All rooms were light and airy and of good proportions.

"Home Sweet Home?"

Much thought had been given to the design of the wards, all of which were on the ground floor, except for two, which were for private patients. They were joined to the centre block by corridors and in an emergency could be separated from the main building quite quickly, by placing special doors across the corridors. Erysipelas cases were treated in four wards, each of two beds and were well isolated from the rest of the hospital.

Each ward had windows on two sides. They were designed to allow any quantity of air required and at any angle. Efficient ventilation dealt with foul air by shutters in the ceiling, known as, 'Tobin's Tubes'. Open fires and hot water pipes were a feature of

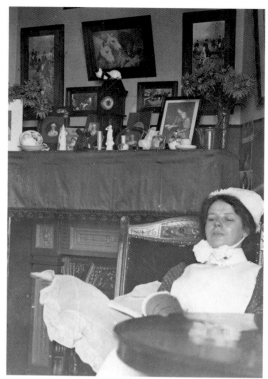

Lovatt

every ward. To the people coming from overcrowded houses, or the 'courts' where water taps and sanitation were shared, these conditions and standards of care and comfort, must have seemed incredible. What pride they must have felt to realise that their own contributions, however small, had achieved such a vast step for-ward for the whole com-munity!

Pretty nurses and Flower Power!

The Sutherland Ward circa 1905

Lovatt

All accidents and injuries from the nearby Florence Colliery were treated in the building facing Belgrave Road and once again, sensible planning was evident. The outpatients' department, a waiting room, surgery, dispensary and a room for dressings, led to a small accident unit, which in turn connected to the operating theatre.

Dr. Davies (1830 - 1902) was Medical Officer of Health for Longton for thirty-five years, as well as medical officer for the Mount Pleasant Hospital and his views were firm on community health. He had stressed the need for a fever hospital and the proper treatment of infectious diseases for many years. He criticised the authorities continuously until there was a gradual, but steady removal of cess-pits resulting in a better system of flushing the sewers. His concern for working mothers, and their children who were put out to nurse and then existed on a diet of bread, water, sago and biscuits was equally strong. "The remedy for ill-health lies with the people," he said.

The New Longton Cottage Hospital must have seemed like a, "Beacon on the Hill," to the patients at this time. The trustees, architects, builders and people were approaching the twentieth century with hope, born of endeavour. The physicians and nurses brought their skills and dedication to each department in this new and wonderful building

*In charge of the Swing!
Sister Stuart and colleagues
circa 1910*

Picture given by Mrs. E. Drew

147

Developments continued with a new operating theatre in 1906, costing £1,220, while free electricity was supplied to the hospital by Florence Coal and Iron Company. There is an interesting item from the diary of Mr. Charles Lovatt, a teacher and historian, the son of J. A. Lovatt, the artist. The notes were made at Hanley Museum in February 1972.

"I saw the key used to open the new operating theatre at Longton Cottage Hospital in 1907. It appeared to be gold-plated. It had a serpent and staff in a thick, filigree pattern at the top of the key. Also on the key was the coloured shield of the Longton Coat of Arms and a coloured picture of Longton Cottage Hospital, looking up Belgrave Road, towards the Church. The case for the key had this inscription:"

W. Andrews (Late W. H. Ashton)
29, Market Street, Longton.
Watchmakers and Jewellers.

The typewritten card in the Museum show case read:

"Silver Gilt key, used by M. J. W. Phillips of Tean
who opened the new theatre."

Private wards were added in 1914 because beds were needed for the wounded from the battlefields. By 1921, an improved and extended Outpatients Department was built on land given by the Trustees of the Duke of Sutherland's estates. It included a Casualty Dressing Room, a theatre for minor operations, a fully equipped Dental Unit, as well as an eye, ear, nose and throat consulting room. These were all served by a new dispensary and sterilising room. The unit was opened by Sir Francis Joseph on October 1st 1923.

During the Depression, quite understandably, donations from the workers virtually ceased and in 1926, the fear of the General Strike, saw the formation of a Linen Guild, by Mrs Hipkins, the wife of the Vicar of Normacot. This provided extra funds and garments for the hospital and even extended to some items of surgical equipment. After her sudden death, due to overwork, in 1928 Mrs Mary Wilkinson, the wife of the headmaster of the Junior School, took responsibility for the organisation of the Guild and its gradual expansion to include some aspects of work in the parish.

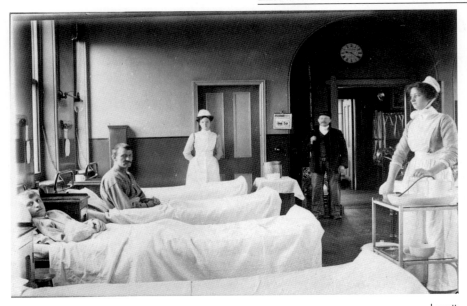

Lovatt

'All Present and Correct!' says the porter.
The Smith Childe Ward 9.20 a.m.

Lovatt

The Laundry:
Coping with the generosity of the Linen Guild!

1930's 'Continuing Excellence'

Photostat of the Hospital Cash Account 1. 10. 1937 to 31. 12. 1938

HOSPITAL CASH ACCOUNT for the Period (15 months) from 1st Oct., 1937 to 31st Dec., 1938

RECEIPTS

	£ s. d.	£ s. d.
To Cash in hand, 30th September, 1937 ...		17 4
,, Balance at Bank, 30th September, 1937		762 7 10
,, General Subscriptions and Donations	817 8 10	
,, Longton Hospital Saturday Committee (including £156 17s. 2d. House-to-House Collection)	425 0 0	
,. Longton Hospital Whist Championship	170 0 0	
		1,412 8 10
,. N.S. Voluntary Hospitals' Contributory Association		3,880 3 6
,, Collieries	419 15 1	
,, Factories	413 10 4	
,, Other Places of Business	297 9 4	
		1,130 14 9
,, Places of Worship		40 18 7
,. Patients' Fees (including £57 12s. 0d. L.M.S. Hospital Fund & £284 5s. 0d. Motor Cases)		2,538 16 3
,, Transfer from Trustees		500 0 0
,, Ward Boxes		50 15 7
,, Club Certificates		13 10 3
,, Sundry Sales and Hire of Articles ...		48 13 6
,, X-Ray Fees		37 4 0
,, Inquest Fees		11 17 0
,, Insurance Money Refunded		1 10 0
,, Bank Interest		8 13 6

PAYMENTS

	£ s. d.	£ s. d.
By Provisions :—		
Greengroceries, Groceries and Bread	597 1 10	
Meat, Chicken and Fish	365 6 10	
Milk	229 10 8	
Spirits	2 19 9	
		1,194 19 1
,, Surgery and Dispensary :—		
Drugs	365 14 2	
Dressings	165 6 11	
Surgical Instruments and Repairs ...	173 16 4	
Pathological Tests	36 1 1	
Oxygen	21 19 8	
X-Ray Films	128 16 2	
		891 14 4
,, Domestic :—		
Laundry Requisites	69 13 2	
Household Requisites	103 19 8	
		173 12 10
,, Establishment :—		
Rates	81 12 11	
Gas and Electricity	189 5 9	
Water	132 11 0	
Telephone	56 12 3	
Insurances	156 8 4	
Ironmongery, Utensils and General Repairs	63 15 5	
Drapery and Uniform	26 0 4	
Painting and Renovations ...	63 7 9	
Repairs to Building	32 18 10	
Carting	2 11 4	
Chimney Sweeping	2 10 0	
		807 13 11
,, Salaries and Wages :—		
Administration	874 15 2	
Nurses	968 18 3	
Masseuse and Locum	251 18 4	
Domestic	396 7 9	
Laundry	175 9 6	
Porters and Gardeners	336 2 8	
		3,003 11 8
,, Miscellaneous :—		
Printing, Stationery and Books ...	80 0 10	
Advertisements	64 3 6	
Stamps, Postage of Parcels, Carriage and Bank Cheque Books	39 15 3	
Ambulance and Taxi Hire	4 16 4	
Locum Fees	1 6 0	
Hospital Payment to Nurses' Pension Fund	123 5 8	
Subscription to British Hospitals' Association	2 2 0	
Sundries	4 7 1	
		319 16 6
,, Transfer to Reserve Deposit Account (for Additional Beds and Heating Apparatus)		3,000 0 0
,, Balance at Bank, 31st December, 1938		1,033 15 2
,, Cash in hand, 31st December, 1938 ...		13 7 5

RECEIPTS TOTAL	PAYMENTS TOTAL
£10,438 10 11	£10,438 10 11

We have examined the above account of Receipts and Payments with the books and vouchers produced to us and certify that it is in accordance therewith.

17th January, 1939.

GEO. S. STODDARD } Honorary
E. S. STODDARD, A.S.A.A. } Auditors.

The expansion and development of the Hospital in the years prior to 1939, was due to the sound financial structure on which its day to day business was based. This enabled the dedicated workforce, both professional and voluntary, to fulfill the high standards of care envisaged by the founder, Adam Clarke.

One of the voluntary workers was Mr. Len Goodwin, chartered accountant and partner in the firm, 'Stoddard, Goodwin and Green," who were auditors to the Hospital. Len had a long association with Longton Cottage Hospital, raising funds in the early years, later becoming acting Secretary following the death of M. E. C. Roberts Esq., and then Vice-chairman of the Hospital Management Committee. The following data from his own official papers, shows some of the development re admissions and days in care from 1892 until 1937.

ADMISSIONS 1892 to 1937

YEAR		Nos ADMITTED	DAYS IN CARE PER CASE	AVERAGE STAY
1892		308	6,582	21+ days
1899		258	6,628	23+ "
1904		341	8,914	26+ "
1906		430	11,273	26+ "
1913		440	7,310	16+ "
1918	*	372	8,390	22+ "
1924		486	7,623	153/5 "
1926	**	626	8,866	14 "
1929		784	10,652	14+ "
1937		968	12,592	13 "

* (Influenza Epidemic) ** (General Strike)

The Report of 1. 10. 1937 to 31. 12. 1938 reveals, even to the modern eye, fifteen months of unrelenting achievement by everyone concerned in the life of the Hospital. The income for these months was £9,675 - 5 - 9 whilst the expenditure totalled £6,391 - 8 - 4. After building a new mortuary, up-dating the kitchen and buying furniture for the newly decorated wards, the expenses incurred were £1,101 - 1 - 5. Ever resourceful, an extension to the Female Ward and the renewal of its heating system, was paid for by the transfer of £3,000 from the reserve account. Individual generosity met the cost of new short wave diathermy equipment given by local benefactors Mr and Mrs F Wildblood, Miss Hudson J.P., and the Rev., Grindley Johnson.

From the very beginning, the Hospital had owed its existence to the fund raising activities of the local community and during the 1930's, inspite of much unemployment in the area, these continued unabated. The Hospital Saturday

Committee raised £425, mainly due to the support of the Alhambra and Alexandra Cinemas, whose owners allowed dancing displays given by Miss Loftus and her pupils to take place on stage. A flourishing Whist Championship Committee realised £170, the North Staffs. Licensed Victuallers gave £130 to the fund, and the Lord Mayor's Coronation Ball donated £40. It is heartening to note that during these difficult years, the miners of pits long gone from our district, Adderley, Mossfield and Parkhall gave £40 to the hospital; it was collected penny by penny over many months by people who valued their own hospital and who were proud to be responsible members of a caring and united community.

The same report included the deaths of professional members of the Board. The Secretary, M. E. C. Roberts Esq., had served for nine years and it was felt that the continuing excellence of the Hospital was a lasting tribute to his memory. The Hon. Consultant Dental Surgeon, J. W. Skae, had given invaluable service by improving dental care and introducing modern dental techniques. Prebendary Codling, Hospital Chaplain, had always given comfort and guidance to those in spiritual need, while the Auditor, M. P. Ferneyhough had brought the highest of standards to the often complex financial affairs of the Hospital.

The list of subscribers for 1937/38 is diverse. Some of the societies are now defunct, but as they played a part in the social history of those times, it is necessary to include them in the story of Longton Cottage Hospital. They included the Hospital Cricket and Football Teams, Potteries Motor Traction Charities, Prudential Assoc. Co. Ltd., Blythe Bridge Carnival Committee, Co-operative Wholesale Soc., Stoke-on-Trent Corporation, Normacot Church of England Linen Guild, the Easter Appeal for Eggs (Matron received 11,350 eggs!) The 'Pound Day Appeal' and the Christmas Appeal.

The Outpatients Report is interesting because in the simplest terms, it gives the numbers of patients treated followed by their total attendances. A clear picture of community needs is apparent in these statistics. Dressings required were 3,400 with attendances numbering 16,739; patients for these would probably be miners, pottery workers and artisans. Similarly, 468 eye cases were admitted with 2,035 attendances recorded. Dental cases inspite of J. W. Skae's skill were 1,291 with an identical number of attendances; perhaps a speedy exit was the order of the day!

Surgical cases numbered 628 with 1,548 further attendances required, whilst the newly improved Ear, Nose and Throat Dept., treated 372 patients with return visits numbering 995. Minor operations and X-Rays had 1,545 and 1,183 patients respectively, each person visiting once. Excellent care for the women of the area was to be found in the gynaecological unit of Mr. Richmond, who had 80 patients during the year. Complications were obviously minimal because only 179 further attendances were recorded. It is obvious that every effort was made to ensure that the services offered to the people of Normacot and Longton were not only of a high standard but also wide ranging; for example, therapeutic massage cases numbered 910 with 7,312 treatments being completed.

After analysing the table of treatments, it is amazing that 9,900 patients were treated during the year by a relatively few physicians and surgeons. The Honorary Medical Staff comprised physicians F. R. Oliver, MRCS., LRCP., A. D. Blakely MD., Ch. B., FRFPSG., A. J. Pollock MB., Ch B., BDPH. The seven surgeons were T. H. Richmond OBE., M.B., (Glasgow) FRCE., E. E. Young MS., (London) FRCS., Consultant H. Hartley MD., (London) FRCS., H. A. Lyth MB., BS., (London) FRCS., L. M. Zinck MD., FRCS., and F. W. Duthie FRCS.

Some of the physicians and surgeons listed had responsibilities in the Outpatients Dept., but others included the Ophthalmic Surgeon, S. McMurray MB., FRCS., the Ear, Nose and Throat Surgeons, G. A. Carter FRCS., E.(Consultant) and M. Gallagher MB., Ch., BAO., (Belfast). The Orthopaedic Surgeon was W. Mitchell Smith MD., CM., (Aberdeen) while R. J. Skae LDS., the son of the late J. W. Skae was the Dental Surgeon. The Matron, Miss Hilda Morris, and the Resident House Surgeon, D. F. Murray MB., B.Ch., BAO., were responsible for the day to day organisation of a rapidly expanding Hospital.

The Ladies Visiting Committee held their meetings at Longton Court House, in Commerce Street; their names evoke memories of well-known and respected families who gave years of service to essential charity work prior to the advent of the Welfare State. They included Mrs George Blair, Mrs J. W. Davies, Mrs S. L. Plant, Mrs W. W. Beswick, Mrs J. W. Skae, Mrs Aspinall, Mrs W. B. Jones, Mrs T Yates, Alderman Miss F. A. Farmer, Mrs A. H. Greatbach, Mrs S. J. Haile and Mrs G Barlow.

During 1936-1937 a, 'Pension Scheme for Senior Members of the Nursing Staff," was discussed and by 1. 1. 1938 the North Staffs Voluntary Hospitals Contribution Assoc., and Central Executive Committee, which represented all Voluntary Hospital Schemes, came into being. All establishment subscriptions were sent to the central office and then distributed amongst the respective Voluntary Hospitals on an agreed basis. Everyone realised that, 'It would benefit every worker".

Once again, Longton Cottage Hospital, was leading the way, not only in excellent patient care, but was now part of a national framework providing secure pensions for its nurses. The post-war transition of these matters into the National Health Service, was already well established at Adam Clarke's, 'Beacon on the Hill."

LONGTON COTTAGE HOSPITAL

Picture given by Mrs. S. Drew

Christmas Carols 1949. The N.H.S., in full swing!

Duncan Stuart, (third row extreme left) the son of Sister Stuart, seen recovering from a serious wrist injury after a motorcycle accident at Meir Cross Roads. Married for only seven weeks and spending Christmas in hospital, he is understandably concerned about the whole situation.

RECENT CHANGES

With the advent of the National Health Service in 1947, the life of the Cottage Hospital continued to evolve and expand. It was in this year that the Childrens' Ward was re-named the, 'Thomas Yates Ward'. At the Dedication Ceremony, the Lord Mayor of the city congratulated all the officials and staff on the homeliness and efficiency of the Hospital, stating that for its size, it was, "second to none."

Nationalisation brought many improvements to medicine, but saw the removal of the 'Longton Donkey'. The first bricks used in the building of Longton Cottage Hospital, were carried by an old donkey, which then remained on the site for the rest of his working life. When he died, the many friends he had made did not want to lose him. With the local expertise of the pottery industry, it was a simple matter to have his bones crushed and then have them made into a China Donkey. He was then placed in the entrance hall in a position of honour until an N. H. S., official ordered his removal. The Aynsley family came to the rescue and kept him in their Pottery Museum. Is he still there? If so, will he be able to return to the hospital he loved?

During the next two decades the work load of all departments increased to a degree which would have astounded the founding fathers. During the 1970's the Ear, Nose and Throat Department had Mr. Carter and Mr. Stuart as consultants, and later Mr. Little. Their work grew as did the scope of the General Surgery Department under the guidance of, Mr. Lawson, the consultant. Mastectomy and amputations were performed in the 1980's and at this time, post-operative cases needing nursing care were transferred from the North Staffs Royal Infirmary.

Before the retirement of the consultant, Mr. Moneypenny, there were four female and four male beds for oncology (cancer) patients. They received daily treatment at the N.S.R.I., but were given nursing care at Longton Cottage Hospital. This service was often for palliative treatment in the terminal stages of the illness.

Longton Cottage Hospital closed for five years so that major changes could be achieved. It was converted from a small, acute hospital to a new style residence for elderly people at a cost of £2.5 million. It was re-opened by H.R.H., The Duchess of Gloucester on 10th November 1992.

Official Re-opening

A homely environment has been created with the same high standards of care given to the residents now, as in the past. There are twenty-eight single rooms and eight double rooms. A complete service to the elderly is given by a dedicated nursing staff. Extras include a hairdressing salon, chiropody, physiotherapy as well as speech and occupational therapy. Attractive seating areas and brightly furnished rooms complete the picture for the residents.

The former Outpatients building has been converted to a Day Unit and Outpatients' Suite. Further expansion of services, notably physiotherapy, are planned for the Millennium.

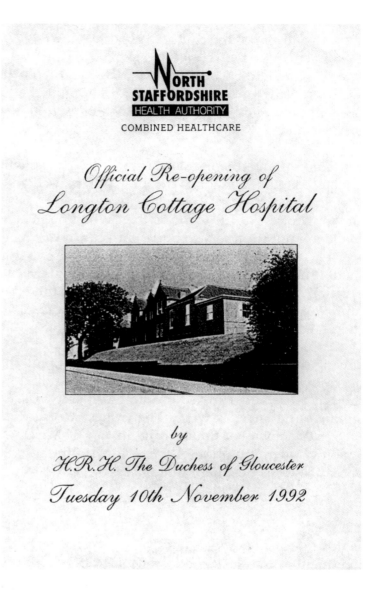

NORTH STAFFORDSHIRE
HEALTH AUTHORITY
COMBINED HEALTHCARE

Official Re-opening of
Longton Cottage Hospital

by
H.R.H. The Duchess of Gloucester
Tuesday 10th November 1992

Today, the outward appearance of the hospital has hardly changed. There is one addition, however, which cannot be seen, but can most certainly be heard. It is a friendly, but industrious ghost in one of the upper rooms of the Central Block! The sound of a treadle sewing machine, with its relentless rhythm, can be heard quite clearly, for extended periods; especially if one is alone! Recently, the ghost has developed a door slamming routine as well as the 'non-

Union' hours spent sewing. Perhaps the extension programme is not progressing quickly enough for this dedicated worker from a by-gone era!

The Reverend Adam Clarke set his own, 'Wheel of Circumstance' in motion in 1869 with his Mount Pleasant Hospital; its further 'spinning' was ensured by the workers, manufacturers and Masonic Brethren who subscribed so selflessly in the pursuit of their ideal. One might suspect that as long as the 'spinning' continues ghostly or otherwise, the hospital will continue to provide care, comfort and hope, for all those who enter its doors.

The corn of plenty, the wine of joy and gladness and the oil of peace were fitting and lasting gifts from the Masonic Brethren.

Lovatt

A Fine Record
Wooden Plaque made by J. A. Lovatt, showing the names of Chairmen from 1886 - 1948. Today, it stands in the entrance to the hospital.

A CENTURY OF MEMORIES

One ship sails East,
　　　and one sails West,
While the self same breezes blow.
'Tis the set of the sails,
　　　and not the gales.
That send them where they go.

Picture given by Mr. C. Turner

Empire Day 1893. Note the white dresses, sashes, paper flags and the elegant teacher! Celebrations took place on the Vicarage lawn after saluting the flag and the singing of national songs at the junction of Normacot and Meir Roads.

Mrs. Wain's shop opposite the Alhambra Cinema circa 1916. A commanding and determined lady who, with her son, Joe, ran the corner shop with military precision. Note the pyramids of polished fruit and the immaculate bedroom curtains.

Picture given by Mr. Dudley Ward

Mrs. Mary Perry (nee Harvey) 'Her own story,'

Mary Perry was born in Normacot in 1902, and when we first met her memory span was accurate and immediate. A bright, friendly and highly intelligent lady, she talked about her life and listed the names of her nine siblings without hesitation. 'Alf, Billy, Mary (herself), Mona, Edith, Joe, Harold, Eric, Millie and Elsie. At the turn of the century, times were hard for many people and my family was no exception. As we grew up, I did the cooking and sewing for all the family; Alf was the, 'Father' and I was the, 'Mother.' Alf was the policeman too, because on summer nights we had to make sure that all the children were at home and in bed, safely. Each night he asked, 'All in order?' and waited for my reply.

I had to sew well because there were many clothes to make or repair; pinafores were needed to cover our long woollen dresses and the boys always wanted shirts and hand knitted stockings. Buttons on their knickerbockers were in need of constant attention and darning torn clothes and socks was a constant chore. Alf made sure that all the shoes were clean and taught the little ones to use the button hook properly. Keeping shoes dry was a problem for every one. We solved it, more or less, by keeping some pork dripping in a jar and Alf brushed the shoes with it as thickly as he could. Clogs were no problem, they were warm and dry, but what a noise they made!

In 1906, when I was four, I started school at Normacot Infants and it was a lovely time in my life. The first class sat on small forms and we played with sand trays, plasticene and coloured, 'bendy' pieces which helped us to make letters; we even had a rocking horse and took it in turn to ride as fast as we liked. When the teacher left the room I was often chosen to be the monitor, so looking back, I must have been well behaved and trustworthy. As we moved up the school we used slates and did so until I was eleven years of age. Paper was a luxury, but slates were useful because you could always rub out your mistakes and start again.

My work at home was hard, but had to be done, so school playtime was a joy to me. I liked the singing games where we joined hands and skipped in a circle; 'The Big Ship Sails on the Ally-Ally-O' and 'On the Mountain stands a Lady'. These songs were special because you had a good chance of being chosen to stand in the middle. Tick and skipping really tired you out and when the summer came, everyone had a whip and top. Hoops were exciting too, we had wooden ones for the girls and iron ones for the boys. We all went home at dinner time, often playing whip and top as we went.

I never played, 'Tip Cat,' but my brothers did. It was played with two sticks, one was sharp at both ends and you put it on the floor; then you hit it at one end to make it fly, and then as quickly as you could, you hit it again, to send it as far forward as possible. The stick which landed in front of all the others was the winner. A lot of skill was needed because you had to be accurate and very quick when you hit the stick for a second time.

I played, 'Diabolo' with string and a cotton reel looped between two sticks; if you wanted to win you had to keep the reel spinning for as long as possible. Leapfrog was good fun; the girls did not play because of their long dresses, but we sometimes joined the boys for marbles and I remember that I had some really good, 'Spotties!' Empire Day was lovely because we stood round the lamp-post in the middle of the road opposite to the Church, where Belgrave, Normacott and Meir roads meet and sang, 'Rule Britannia'. Lots of parents came to hear us and some helped to push the piano to and from the Big School. It would be impossible today with all the traffic; even now, it's hard to realise how quiet it was in those days, when to me, every day at school seemed happy and sunny. As soon as we went home we had to be grown up and take a lot of responsibility.

When I was eight I went to the Junior School; our new teachers were Miss Sutton, Miss May Allen, Miss Ethel Hibberts, Miss Mamie Hall (Ophelia Jane's niece). The girls were taught downstairs, the boys were upstairs and Mr. William Wilkinson was the Headmaster. We were weighed and measured on the first day and it was discovered that I was only four feet one inch tall, at eight!

'The Way Down to the Big School' circa 1910

Lovatt

The houses and the crossroads remain today, but the school was demolished in 1956.

Note the Police House on the corner and the snow-white aprons and dress. Is the child in the 'bassinette' facing up Meir Road part of a general photo-call?

In 1912, we had the Pit Strike, which went on for twelve weeks; it was a dreadful time. Mother was in bed having her eighth child Eric and there was neither work nor money to be had. My father was proud and would not accept the, 'charity' of a local soup kitchen. Then, the Church Schools decided that somehow they would provide meals; breakfast, dinner and tea. Father had always been a good worker, and normally, he always put some money by so my mother had never gone without a week's wages until now. Soon, father had to go coal picking at Florence Colliery, to make sure that we had a fire and were able to cook. Mr. Wilkinson insisted that our family went for food, including those not of school age.

The children gathered near to the iron staircase where there was some shelter from the bitterly cold weather and fresh tea was brewed in an out building in the yard. We had to take our own plates, basins, cups or mugs; the boys went to the Infant School and the girls to the Junior School. I remember that we had real cocoa, sausage and mash, bread and toast with 'dripping.' Kindness and care was shown to the children, many of whom were cold and ill, during that long and frightening time of unemployment.

A lot of children caught diptheria after the strike; families often hid the illness because of the unjust stigma of being dirty, when it was really linked with the results of poverty. The doctor's fee for coming was two shillings and sixpence and if there was no money, death was the result. The only effective treatment was the swabbing of throats and fresh air at Bucknall Isolation Hospital. Bonds with the family were often broken when children were away from home for weeks or months. Alf and I were at Bucknall together, where everyone was kind and the food was quite good. Alf was a clever boy and he was dreadfully upset when he missed the scholarship examination for Longton High School, while he was ill. There were no second chances in those days and although Mr. Wilkinson sent a letter to the Board, Alf knew that he was, 'out'. Inspite of this, Alf went to see him, just in case there was a second chance, and he was given sixpence which he shared with me when he came home. With my three-pence I bought some silks and a crochet hook and asked my Mother to teach me how to use them. Alf always found learning easy. During the First World War he served on the Russian front near Lake Onega and years later when he retired, he studied for his 'O' level examination in Russian and passed with distinction. So, who knows what he might have achieved if he had been given a second chance?

Lovatt

Extra curricular activity at Normacot C of E Junior School circa 1912. The huts in the school yard from which hot drinks and food were available during the strike are just visible.

Inspite of all this, there were happy times in Normacot especially at Christmas when we took our turkey to Billing's bakehouse at the end of Furnace Road; years later Mrs Sherratt kept it and her bread and cakes were lovely. On the opposite corner in Queensberry Road was Bromley's fruit and vegetable shop, so we could do all our shopping close to home.

Chaplin Road was different when I was a child; we only saw bicycles, a few pony and traps and the luxurious carriages of the manufacturers which we thought were wonderful. The Duke of Sutherland made sure that in the summer, the dust on the roads was kept down by horse drawn carts each carrying a large tank of water. Sprinklers were attached behind and they took half a day to go up and down Chaplin Road and do the job properly. Often, tar was put on the road and people would drag a piece of string or a cloth in it while it was fresh. Then if their baby had a cold, they would let it breathe the tar fumes, using it like eucalyptus today.

Everyone has so much now; money, jobs, modern medicines and yet families are split, leaving children unhappy and uncertain. I'm glad that I lived my life when I did, because inspite of hardship and a lack of many things, we all belonged together.

Sarah Frances (Sally) Ralphs (nee Daniels.)

Born in Melville Road, she said,

"Everyone felt safe in Normacot, but parents were strict during the days following the First World War, and always fetched their daughters from Guides and birthday parties; even the older girls had to be at home by 9.30 pm. Some of my family worked at the, 'Alhambra', my mother and aunt in the kiosk selling tickets and sometimes they were usherettes. My cousins, Bill and George Broad were the Commissionaires, and being tall, they looked really handsome in their uniforms of crimson with gold braid trimmings. During the First World War I had whooping cough very badly and went into Longton Cottage Hospital. A side effect of the infection led to badly ulcerated eyes and I couldn't see properly for nearly six weeks but I had wonderful care from Mr. McMurray, the consultant. I hated being poorly because a lot of the 'cures' were dreadful. Every Friday night, we had a bath and hairwash and were then dosed with sickly tasting Syrup of Figs. For a sore throat, olive oil and raspberry vinegar was not too bad, if you were quick about it!

While I was in hospital a Zeppelin came over, searching for Shelton Bar, I suppose. I heard the crash and explosion and told mother about it. I learned later that her return train from Normacot to Blythe Bridge had stopped in Meir Tunnel for about an hour, until all danger had passed.

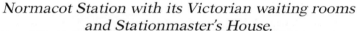

Normacot Station with its Victorian waiting rooms and Stationmaster's House.

The Station, Normacot.

52T

When I was growing up, there were so many shops in Normacot, not only in the main streets, but in every side street too. Dale's grocers shop was on the corner of Normacot and Uttoxeter Roads, with Dr. Carrington's Surgery directly opposite. Lowe's wet fish shop was just below Dale's with an oatcake and pikelet shop next door and Mill's Bakery just behind. Farmer's Chemists was in the middle of a row of small shops facing the surgery. Miss Sutton's dressmakers, Grindley's Ladies outfitters and Gordon's, selling wool and embroidery silks, were lovely shops catering for a good clientele. Joe Wain and his mother had their sweets and tobacco shop on the corner of Spring Road with Griffin's selling the same things just opposite. The Co-op was the, 'Big Store', with its dairy, meat and grocery departments and of course its Dividend Book for each customer! There were no superstores and so there was plenty of trade for everyone. We even had our own Toffee Factory, Garbett's in Normacot Road, near to Queensberry School, so you see, in its own way, Normacot had everything we wanted.

Trentham Hall and Gardens

The high spot of the year, apart from Newhall Mission Anniversary which was wonderfully organised with concerts, outings and of course new dresses and shoes, was Trentham Thursday. It was always in Wakes Week after Bank Holiday Monday and the children from all the Potteries towns could go. Some families had ponies and traps, some had carts, even coal carts were used while others came by canal boat. There was great excitement because in those days the Park and Gardens at Trentham were not open to the public and everyone knew that they were visiting the Duke of Sutherland at his home. It always seemed to be warm and sunny on that day and the Normacot children felt 'special' because the Duke had done so much for them building their church, their school and in many cases, their homes. Now they were off to enjoy picnics and games at Trentham Hall; many walked there and didn't mind; it was fine going, but pitiful to see them walking home after their long day. It was better to go by trap or cart, especially if it was a full day's work or 'half-time' at school next day!"

Emmy Williams (nee Hurst) Born 1902.

"As a girl, I often worked at the Vicarage; it was just like going home, but to a good home, as everyone was so kind. I could visit at any time and often helped with the washing up. I always had a good meal there and although my mother's meals were nice and she did her best, times were difficult. I remember that the Reverend Hipkins was of middle height and rather stout; he was reserved, as befitted his station, and always used a walking stick for his visits in the parish. Mrs Hipkins worked very hard and did lots of extra things with the Church Societies and Guilds. I loved dusting her bedroom and tidying the necklaces on her dressing table. They were beautiful and probably very expensive. I knew that were no others like them in Normacot. Once, I was brave enough to try one on and it looked lovely!

The housekeeper, Ellen Thorpe, was kindness itself to me; she was always so gentle and knew that we didn't have a lot at home. She returned to Yorkshire every year to visit her family, because the Vicar and his wife made sure that she kept in regular touch with her relatives, especially as she had been at the Vicarage for so many years. I remember her as a tall, heavily built matronly figure; dignified at all times.

*Normacot Vicarage.
(previously the
Furnace Inn)
Well trimmed lawns,
neatly clipped ivy and
tidy borders at the turn
of the century.*

Outside, the Vicarage was beautiful. The lawns were smooth and green and with the borders full of flowering shrubs, it looked like a small park, which sometimes I had all to myself! There was always a feeling of quietness and space. I loved the latticed windows and the heavily studded front door. To me, the walk up the long drive was a pleasure, whatever the season.

The school and the Church saw my family through hard times, especially during the First World War. I like this picture, because although the war is not over, the little girl is smiling and the Church looks beautiful."

A Happy Easter! 1917.

Lovatt

Nancy Henshall (nee Locker) of Star and Garter Road.

"As I get older, childhood memories become much clearer, and the memory of the Infants School Headmistress, the often dreaded Miss Ophelia Jane Hall, is etched most vividly on my mind, even today. She lived at the corner of Lightwood Road and Fir Tree Road with her niece, Miss Edie Collett, who was also a teacher.

Miss Hall had quite a masculine appearance and strode about, usually in the middle of the road, wearing a black cloak and a black Homberg hat. She also rode a bicycle and to the amazement of many people in Normacot, wore a divided skirt. Some small boys said that they had seen her smoking a cigar and after much discussion had decided from the wealth of their knowledge that she must be a man in disguise! Inspite of her strictness at school and her astonishingly strong personality, I always found her to be kind and generally fair to all concerned. However, whatever the occasion, she would not tolerate interference from anyone. I remember her standing outside the Infants' School before classes, with one hand raised, ready to stop any oncoming traffic in Meir Road. This, inspite of the fact that there might have been one car in Normacot at the time; other traffic would have included a few ponies and traps, horse drawn carts and some bicycles. Even the trams only used the Longton to Uttoxeter Road. When questioned by the Vicar over these extra duties, Miss Hall was adamant that, "They must learn road safety," and that was that!

Miss Ophelia Jane Hall, Headmistress. She would often, 'tour' the streets at dusk to make sure that all the children were in the house and on their way to bed!

Classroom punishment was swift, usually a smack on the knuckles with a jam spoon. Another punishment was being made to stand in the corner, but Miss Hall always made sure that the little children faced the front, in case they felt lonely. In the event of a child being really naughty they were addressed in a loud voice by their full name. That was enough to restore order! Morning assembly was held in the big room which was the middle one of three. In the winter, this was really enjoyable, because the roaring fire was welcome to children who had left a home with an empty hearth and just a piece of bread with dripping or jam for breakfast. The fireguard often held items of clothing drying out on a rainy morning or after an 'accident' on the way to school! At every assembly, Miss Hall asked, "Did you help your mother this morning?" and of course she wanted details. She was well aware of conditions in many homes and also how hard mothers of large families had to work, both at home and often at the pot bank.

Certain days stand out in my mind, Empire Day, in particular. Everyone loved the celebrations, because on the big day we had white dresses and paper flags. We joined the older pupils from the Junior School and walked, in procession, to the Vicarage garden where the Reverend Hipkins and his wife made us welcome. The retinue was led by Miss Britannia, with Miss India and Miss Africa and children depicting all the other countries of our Empire, following behind. Many patriotic songs and anthems were sung while Miss Britannia sat on her throne. Then we all danced round her, singing more songs until it was time for each one of us to step forward and salute the flag. To us, the Union Jack seemed huge as it swirled above our heads. This was the part I liked best, because when we saluted, it made us proud to be British and we knew that Normacot was just as important as anywhere else in the world.

I remember 'changing' from an Infant into a Junior very clearly. It was September, and after morning assembly, Miss Hall asked who was going to win a scholarship and of course, everyone's hand went up! In a voice which would brook no interference, she said, "You'll make the grade" and then led the way down Meir Road to the Big School. Her black cloak billowed behind her and we followed, holding hands in two's. This school seemed huge, with its two storeys, a dark entrance porch and two playgrounds. For the first time we were separated from the boys at playtime. Mr. William Wilkinson, the Headmaster, was there to meet us and we went into the big, middle room downstairs and then to our classes. Our new life had begun; strict discipline and tests each day when we reached scholarship age. The school was a village school and we knew that underneath the discipline there was kindness and concern for the children and their families; I really enjoyed being taught there.

I appeared in one play, 'The Wedding of the Painted Doll'. I was the Doll and wore a white dress and my best friend was the Bridegroom. We were taught by our class teacher Miss Ella Wilkinson. First, we performed it for the whole school and then later in Church in front of the congregation. Mr. Stanley Mitchell played the piano for us and it was his fault that I fell hopelessly in love at the age of eleven! He was so attractive and handsome. I even wanted to wear rimless glasses, as he did, so that I could be a real soul-mate; unfortunately, all my friends felt the same way about him too. Inspite of these distractions, there was much success in our examinations, with many of us going to Longton High School; Miss Hall's predictions had indeed come true!

Picture given by Miss M. Webb

Standard II with their teacher, Mr. Stanley Mitchell,
who was later awarded the M.B.E., for his services to educaton.

Back Row ?,?,?,John Beswick,?,?,?, Teacher Mr. Mitchell
3rd Row ?,?, Gratton, Nancy Wyatt, Nancy Birks, Marjorie Webb,
Bertha Bailey, ?.
2nd Row John Barnes, John Lowndes, ?, Nancy Hammersley,
Nellie Brindley, Irene Sutton, Nancy Locker, ?, Ronnie Smith.
Front ?, ? Skelhern, John Webb, Lewis Barnett, Peter Lowndes,
Douglas Dale, ?.

Stanley Mitchell MBE., 1906

The First Headmaster of Blurton County Junior School 1947-67

'Memories of a Young Teacher in the 1920's'

Mr. William Wilkinson, Headmaster of Normacot C of E School, was a 'wizard' at teaching Arithmetic and a grand person to work for!

In the days of 'Chalk and Talk' he was the perfect example of those in the profession who would experiment with new ideas, but always in a controlled way. He retained that which had stood the test of time and then used those elements of the new which he found to be superior to the old.

Children recited the multiplication tables, but this was mainly as a 'refresher course' to help them to know and understand numbers.

He would place 12 counters on the table and ask the children to divide them into groups of three and then to count how many groups were made in that way. They did likewise with groups of 4 and 6 and in this way they would DISCOVER the basis of numeration.

Soon counters became unnecessary and the multiplication tables (which were also the division tables!) were well and truly learnt. At this point the children realised that multiplication was really continuous addition and division continuous subtraction. Pupils revelled in this 'adventure-discovery' and were more than ready for the informal introduction to square-root as a grouping of (3 x 3) equalling 9 which then became $\sqrt{9=3}$

When 'WW' presented his mathematical fun-game of 'Chinese Arithmetic' the children were full of confidence and could hardly wait. He called it 'Wun-Lung-Sum!' This gave practice in mechanical processes underlying and extending the previous use of tables and counters.

For example, 243 x 9 = 2187. This had to be proved by 9 successive subtractions (243 from 2187 = 1944) then (243 from 1944) continuing until zero was reached. There were few uncertainties or inhibitions from the children because of excellent planning and intelligent teaching which resulted in the easy understanding of each mathematical step taken.

Ahead of his time, once again, WW introduced 'Specialisation' in the days when one teacher was usually responsible for all the subjects taught to his or her own class. This was unsatisfactory for both pupils and teachers, so WW deployed his staff to make the most of their individual talents and changed the time-table to benefit everyone.

In the days of large classes of 55 or more pupils, he introduced the 'Vertical System' whereby those of similar aptitude but possibly of different ages were grouped in columns for special work. These columns radiated from the high chair and desk of the teacher where the view of the room was excellent! Again, a controlled experiment which was useful for large numbers in the old elementary system; it lasted only a short time at Normacot because WW found it inferior to existing methods.

Many years later some Government Inspectors were keen to introduce their new idea of 'Vertical' teaching and appeared to want it to be adopted within the modern system. At a packed meeting, I distinguished myself by suggesting that if this method were adopted as the norm then, "Everyone would be vertical except the teacher!"

At Normacot, History was taught from the aspect of society as a whole, with trends and achievements being of prime importance. Dates were merely the 'pegs' from which to hang the information. The effect of history on peoples' lives was always stressed; Newton (gravity) Watt (steampower) Stephenson (steam engine).

WW had an 'eye' for any subject not usually taught in the elementary schools; he soon discovered that I knew some trigonometry! Consequently, it was not long before I sallied forth with a small group of children, a theodolite and some 45 degree set squares to make good use of the isosceles triangle. We measured the height of trees, buildings, the width of a stream, nothing was safe from our endeavours at 'discovery-learning!'

When teaching Geography, WW made us realise that young children are often bewildered by concepts of scale and distance. He maintained that flat, isolated maps were confusing, sometimes meaningless when continents and oceans were studied. At Normacot, the globe was the key to understanding relative size and distance in their simplest terms.

The younger children began with familiar places. Maps or diagrams were made which started from their own home and traced their journey to school;

the church, Post Office, Grocer's and Butcher's were marked clearly. Later, pottery factories, Florence Colliery and the Railway Station would be added as the child's perception developed. At this point Geography and History became as one when the inter-dependence of clay, coal, pottery was understood.

Photograph: Normacot Junior Mixed School 1925
Mr. Stanley Mitchell aged 19

Picture given by Mr. S. Mitchell

Back Row: Millie Blagg, Bentley, ?, Hakesley, John Beswick, Jack Floyd, George Brown, Leese, Hawkins.
4th Row: ?, Marie Gerrard, ?, Peggy Elsmore (with slate), Jean Drakeford, Elsie Simpson(?), Gwen Bryan, ?, Lily Smith
3rd Row: Tom Byatt, Marion Reeves, ?, Millie Brittain, ?, Edna Flynn, Edna Merriman, Joyce Proctor, Ada Bough (later a teacher with Mitchell at Blurton).
2nd Row: Colclough (Twin), ?, Betty Charlesworth, ?, ?, Dorothy Goodfellow, Ethel Blagg.
Front Row: Woolley, Oliver Bryan, Mountford, Cope Twins, ?, ?, Colclough (Twin).

WW was a talented man; he was a good violinist an excellent player of draughts and chess. During my five years at the school I never won at chess and triumphed only once at draughts! Being well versed in Greek and Latin he knew the advantages of the correct use of the Latin prefix and suffix in grammar, spelling and conversation.

Spelling was always taught in context, never in lists of un-related words and subsequently linked with reading, sentence construction and essays. From the beginning an essay had to be planned and an extra piece of paper was always supplied for this purpose! The introduction had to contain a 'telling' sentence to attract the interest of the reader while each paragraph had to present a salient point which then led to a final summary.

As the child's skills developed a regular lesson in calligraphy was given. This required an 80 degree slope to the right so that it's flow was easily legible and pleasing to the eye; pot-hooks were always included! His own script was superb, whether on paper or on the blackboard.

"A good reader will spell correctly and write coherently", was his maxim. This could only be achieved successfully with a degree of home learning and where possible, parents were expected to co-operate.

William Wilkinson
on his retirement in 1934.

After years of 'progressive' teaching it is heartening to know that many of these methods achieved by William Wilkinson are returning to favour as proven successes. They provided the children of Normacot School with a sound education which would see them through life and have a most beneficial bearing on their future, whatever that future might hold.

Sentinel

Frank Redman, Ludwell Road, Normacot

"Scouting helps to shape the character of boys the world over. With the motto 'Service to Others', they make friends for life".

Although in his late 80's, Frank Redman recalls with clarity, how Normacot scouting began in the early years of the twentieth century.

"Because of the enthusiasm of Father T. L. Murray of St. Mary and St. Chad's Church in Sandford Hill, Longton Scout group was formed in 1908 and inaugurated in 1910.

Soon, the teachers and pupils of Normacot C of E Sunday School and Bible Class, became interested in these 'goings-on' and by 1912 they wanted to start a Troop of their own. A small delegation, George Dale, John Rhodes, Alf Lack and Bert Bentley, went to see Father Murray for details and guidance. On the strength of his advice matters went ahead very quickly".

In those days, Normacot was a real community and soon many people were involved. All those interested met in the school playground. Uniforms were needed, so the ladies made shorts from cast-off trousers, while boys who were better off paid two-pence per week for hats and shirts.

"All scouts need a staff so we went to Hill's Nurseries who sold us ash poles, trimmed them and then we brought them home on a hand cart loaned by John Dawson, the undertaker. Rupert Johnson and Bert Bentley were in charge of the operation".

By 1913, everything was ready, so a troop was formed and registered later. Their first meeting place was in the Infants' School under their first Scoutmaster, George Dale; Assistant Scoutmasters were Arthur Hill and Rupert Johnson. A detailed training programme was arranged by the Headmaster of Queensberry Evening School, Mr. Finney, while George Dale subscribed to the magazine, 'Scouting for Boys' for up to the minute news!

"The first boys in the Troop were Reg Webberley, Bill Harvey, Reg Hobson, Alf Harvey, Bill Brain, Arthur Brookfield, Aaron Walker, Harold Jones, Thomas Kent, Billy Blackburn and the twins Roy and Robert Jamieson, Harry Warren, Alf Hawley and Ted Sollom. Tests on scouting were given by Mr. Finney, all the candidates did well, so they organised their first camp at Rhyl in 1914. This was the week when war was declared!"
According to Frank, the Territorials, who shared the camp were called to duty. They immediately commandeered all the trains, leaving the Normacot Scouts in the camp for an extra week with a good supply of rations.

They had a wonderful time at Rhyl. Thanks to Mrs Hipkins, they had bugles and drums and were able to rehearse outside their tents before the daily Church Parades took place. The silk flag used at their first camp had pride of place in Normacot Church, but was destroyed completely in the fire of October 1997.

Nothing could stop the Normacot Scouts; their numbers increased and inspite of money being scarce they had regular camps. In those days, transport, other than by rail, was minimal, so sites were chosen with care. Sale Lodge Farm at Salt and Sexton's Field at Fulford were popular venues, as were Brocton and Cannock Army Training Camp. However, by 1919, the picture had changed because boys who had joined in 1913 were conscripted towards the end of the war. Many were killed in action, or wounded. Some succumbed to the gas attacks of 1918.

However, rescue was at hand when the sixteen year old Herbert Harvey transferred from the Edensor Troop. For more than twenty years, he helped to ensure the success of the 7th Longton Scouts, later the Duke of Sutherland's Own. He held them together at a crucial time and rose through the ranks from Cub Master, Scout Master to become Group Scout Master and Camp Commissioner at Kibblestone.

Beeston Castle
1919
L to R Fred Stubbs,
Billy Blackburn,
Harry Shenton
Herbert Harvey
(Drum), Cecil
Stubbs, Ted Sollom
Alf Hawley
(emigrated to S.
Africa and then
started a Scout
Troop!) and Douglas
Hawley (no relation)

Bentley

Frank remembered that "A suitable meeting place had always been a problem. Our Troop was so popular that boys didn't want to leave and, as numbers grew, we formed a Rover Group. Imperial Headquarters then decided that in due course we should progress to having a Venture Scout Unit for sixteen to twenty-year olds. Luckily, we were given a room at Garbett's Toffee Factory, near to the junction of Lower Spring Road and Normacott Road.

What we really wanted was a home of our own. After a lot of hard work, this was achieved in 1924 and we moved in with all debts paid.

Our Scout Hut was in Star and Garter Road, just before the white cottage, near to what is now Chelmorton Avenue. It measured 60' x 20' and cost £50. In those days land in Wardill's sandpit was priced at three shillings per square yard! I remember that the Junior School Kitchen garden had been on the site of our new hut, when Mr. Wm Wilkinson was Headmaster. It was never 'raided' because by morning he would have known the names of the culprits!

After paying our debts we could only afford to have our annual camp in Degg's Fields and we held our Church Service and Parade at St. James' Church.

All our activities needed money and we were prepared to work hard for it. One pound was needed for one week in camp, so fundraising was a serious matter. When we collected money, we always made sure that 'T. C.' Wild's St. Mary's Factory was our first stop because he always gave us £1. We knew that other factories like J. H. Barlow and George Blair would then do the same.

Door to door collections were really hard work, but we had a special poem printed to push through the letter-boxes. It usually worked miracles and I've often wondered who wrote it."

"To live up to our motto 'Service to Others' we kept the Vicarage lawn and the Churchyard neat and tidy throughout the seasons. People knew how to behave in those days and there were no damaged gravestones to be seen. The large oak tree sheltered the graves close by and no-one would have left litter about at any time. Normacot Scouts worked so hard at Kibblestone Camp that we were known as the, 'Chain Gang' and our record of achievement is worth looking at, if you visit the camp."

Normacot Scouts' Bazaar

Nov. 27th and 29th, 1924.

If good friend, with willing mind,
To render help you feel inclined,
For Normacot Scouts' Bazaar,
Suitable the following are :—
Blacklead, blacking, starch and soap,
Cotton, worsted, twine and rope,
Pins and needles, inks and pens,
Geese and turkeys, ducks and hens ;
Books and photographic views
Some obliging friend might choose ;
Others might the rather vote
Coins of gold, or five pound note.
Send us, if you will, a ham,
Jars of jelly or of jam,
Sacks of flour or chests of tea,
Either will most welcome be.
Walking sticks and washing tubs,
Window plants and garden shrubs.
Shoes and slippers, boots and socks ;
Sheets and blankets, watches, clocks,
Tea and coffee, bread and cheese ;
All of these are sure to please.
Crochet-work of course will do,
Articles in wool-work too,
Children's robes of every kind,
Rapid sale will always find.
Dolls unclothed, or neatly dressed,
Girls are certain to request.
While to please the little boys,
We shall need a host of toys.
Ornamental fretwork sells,
Perfumes sweet to suit the belles ;
If your choice be none of these,
Kindly send us something, please.

P.S.—The Scoutmaster, Officers and all the the Bazaar workers are anxious to receive numerous and early responses to the above appeal.

A Scout will call on you during the next few days.

178

Scouting gave us wonderful experiences and opened up the world to boys coming from a small village. We went to the Prince of Wales Jamboree at Wembley Stadium in 1924, while some Venture Scouts went to Denmark for the International Jamboree. All the Normacot Troop attended the 1929 Jamboree at Birkenhead and we actually saw the great man, Baden-Powell.

The first River Crew was formed by the Longton Division in 1931 and Bill Harvey and I were members. The Jubilee of King George Vth in 1935 was memorable when scouts lit beacons across the country, ours was the biggest in the area!

War overtook us once more in 1940 and we shared our Scout Hut with the A. R. P. Some of our boys and young men were conscripted but we struggled on and reformed after the war.

Picture given by Mr. F. Redman

Scouts for Life: Building the Dale Shelter
L to R Harry Blundred, Ray Povey, Harold Thompson,
Frank Redman, Herbert Harvey (his Grandfather was the Town Crier!),
Les Hollins. Foreground: John Lowndes.

In 1954, we felt that a tribute should be paid to our founder, George Dale, to mark his devoted service to Normacot Scouts. So, after much discussion and planning we built the 'Dale Shelter' at Kibblestone Camp, and a good job we made of it too! We made an appeal for £150 which was the approximate cost of the building; finances were looked after by Harry Blundred, Tom Clare and Fred Tunnicliffe."

Fifty years of Scouting was celebrated in 1962. The festivities lasted a week and in the Parish Magazine of October, the Rev. Lawrence Williams wrote, "As part of their birthday celebrations the Scout and Cubs invite you all to a really good bonfire and firework display in the Church House grounds on November 5th at 7.30 pm., Parents, friends and congregation are all welcome. Refreshments, (hot dogs etc) will be available!"

Frank Redman remembered the Jubilee Dinner held in the Parish Hall for one hundred people and Mr. Marshall Amor, who had given a life-time to scouting, was the principal speaker. One of his stories ran thus:

"An eight year old boy was asked by his mother if he would like a ginger pop. After a moment's reflection, he said, "Well anything would be better than the old buffer we've got!"

After the celebrations, Rev. Lawrence Williams reflected further on the Scout movement, "Every month there is a meeting in the Church House of a group of men whose common link is that they were boys in the Normacot Scouts some forty or fifty years ago. Quite recently, a room in the Church House has been transformed by their voluntary labour to achieve a Headquarters for the movement."

"The years pass so quickly" said Frank, "but I do remember how hard Rev. Duncan Leak worked for the scouts and Rev. Beaver was very keen indeed. They both wanted a really active Church Pack because this was important for the 1973 celebrations for sixty years of scouting in Normacot. A year later, Herbert Harvey received an inscribed silver dish for his service during those years."

By 1975, matters had moved quickly and a permanent Scout and Guide Headquarters was built in the grounds of the now demolished Church House.

"It cost more than £5,000 to build and was held between the Parochial Church Council and the Scout Association Trust Corporation. The agreement was to last until 2024, so it will see me out!" said Frank.

Amongst his many mementos and awards for Scouting, Frank is most proud of the 'Medal of Merit' awarded for his record of unbroken service, and which was presented to him by Commissioner Peter Moxon.

Today, as the Millennium approaches, Frank had one regret. "Stamina, or the lack of it! When we went to the Alexandra Park Rally in 1921, we took an early train to London. We had a good meal at the Y. M. C. A., at Euston followed by a charabanc tour of London. This was a surprise treat arranged for us by Wallace Copeland and then we went to the Rally. It was a huge affair and went on for hours. At midnight, we caught the train for Stoke and then in the early hours, we walked home to Normacot!

Programme: Opening Celebrations of Normacot Scout and Guide Headquarters 26th July 1975.

PROGRAMME

WELCOME: HERBERT HARVEY Esq.
Chairman Normacot B.P. Guild of Old Scouts
Former Cubmaster, Scoutmaster and Group Scoutmaster

OPENER: MARSHALL AMOR Esq., J.P.,
Former Divisional Secretary, Stoke-on-Trent and Newcastle Scout Association.

PRAYERS: The Rev. CHRISTOPHER BEAVER, Chaplain

RESPONSE:

Mrs. MARY YATES, J.P.
County Commissioner, Staffordshire Girl Guides Association.

PETER MOXON Esq.
County Commissioner, Staffordshire Scout Association

PRESENTATION OF AWARDS

Simultaneous DISPLAYS AND EXHIBITIONS presented by members of the Group, Units and Guild, with the guidance of RON HARRIS, Scout Leader, JEANETTE BEAVER, Guide Leader, MADELINE HARRIS, Cub Scout Leader, JOAN PEDLEY, Brownie Guide Leader, and their Assistant Leaders.

REFRESHMENTS served at the same time in the Parish Hall

CAMP FIRE: The Singing led by The Rev. DUNCAN LEAK, Former Group Scout Leader.

PARTNERSHIP

The opening of the new Scout and Guide Headquarters in Normacot starts a new chapter in a long history. The building is a venture of partnership between brothers and sisters who have long worked in parallel, though only recently in close conjunction.

PAST:

There are some present who well remember the beginnings of Scouting in Normacot, when George Dale founded the Troop in 1913, and more who can recall Mrs. Hipkins as Guide Captain some 10 years later. Both organisations, with their junior sections, have had sponsorship, a good deal of leadership, and the use of various buildings —schools, Old Vicarage and hall—from the same Parish Church.

Even in the long years when Scouts and Cubs met in a building of their own, from the 20's to the 50's, Guides were frequent visitors on many social occasions and, of course, Church Parades have always been a joint activity.

PRESENT:

Ever since that former building 'in the sand pits' ceased to be available, there has been the intention of having a new Headquarters and for the past five years the Guides and Brownie Guides and their supporters have been involved with their brothers in planning it and raising the necessary funds.

At times, as prices have risen, the project seemed a forlorn dream. Had it been known the cost would eventually be well over £5,000 that dream might never have become fact. And had it not been for the enthusiasm of a few, willingness of some to give time and skill unstintingly, and the generosity of many, it would have been an impossible pipe-dream.

We never seemed to be tired, they were happy days and we had lots of friends in Scouting.

Who could ask for more?"

George Richard Donkin 1908 - 1986

The last Headmaster of Normacot

No-one could have brought more dedication and endeavour to the declining years of Normacot Church of England Junior School, than George Richard Donkin. A man of quiet dignity and strength of character, he felt a deep responsibility for the children and staff in his care; especially, when facing a series of professional difficulties, soon after his appointment.

Educated at Longton High School, he gained entrance to King Alfred's College, Winchester, for Teacher Training Studies. He was a keen debator in the College Society and as a voluntary tutor became involved with the Education Courses for the inmates of Winchester Prison. His widow, Rhoda, remembered that George was surprised by two things during his prison visits. Firstly, there were, 'degree men,' serving sentences and secondly, he found the prison food much superior to that which was served at the college!

Prior to his headship, he taught at a number of City schools, including Cook Street (Fenton) and Queensberry Road (Normacot) when Mr. Brandrick was the Headmaster. One of George's main interests, was Esperanto, and as an early member of the local Society he worked steadily to make it available in schools where foreign languages were not taught.

On his appointment at Normacot, George Donkin inherited a school where dedicated teaching, resulting in excellent 'scholarship' success, had been the norm for many years.

However, he also inherited an ageing and unsafe building. Mrs Donkin said, "One Monday morning, just before school started, George saw a huge crack in a classroom ceiling; on further inspection, there was evidence of serious structural faults in other parts of the school. All the children were sent home and George informed the Education Department, in Hanley, immediately." Help from Lichfield Diocese and the Local Education Authority was needed, desperately. However, nothing was forthcoming and any evidence of forward planning, did not appear to be on the agenda.

The school was moved to the Technical College site in Trentham Road (now demolished). The sorry saga of the gradual demise of Normacot C of E Junior School had begun.

In spite of falling numbers and the change of site, the parents and children were loyal to the school. They realised that all the staff were experienced teachers. They included Mr. William (Bill) Wilkinson, who was well versed in the requirements for scholarship examinations, and Mrs. Ratcliffe, who had served the school for many years. She was an excellent class teacher and as many will remember, a strict disciplinarian.

Miss Eve Rowley, a sincere and dedicated teacher, was also a member of the Workers' Education Association and had written a history of the Longton Branch. As a co-author, with George Donkin, a 'History of Barlaston School 1680 - 1962' was produced which was a scholarly and detailed account of a unique village school.

Another loyal member of staff was Mr. Walter C. Williams. He had much experience in teaching for the 11+ examination and also took a keen interest in sport. He gave many hours of his own time to coach boys and girls for the Town and City Sports where they competed successfully. As Treasurer of the North Staffordshire and District Branch of the National Union of Teachers, he served with distinction, later becoming Vice Chairman of the Central Council of the Teachers' Benevolent Fund.

As is evident from these details, all the staff had distinguished themselves in both education and professional service. Incredibly, nothing was done to ensure the scholastic future of Christian families in Normacot, despite the wishes of the parents, children and priest, that the school should continue to exist. Gradually, the numbers on roll began to fall. The children were no longer in the heart of the village and without them, the church clubs and activities began to founder.

George Richard Donkin on his 74th Birthday in 1982.

Normacot School closed in 1956 and George Donkin became Headmaster of Longton Church of England Primary and Infants School. Five years later he was appointed Headmaster of St., Mary's School, Bucknall.

His time at St. Mary's was both happy and successful. He was consulted over many aspects of the new school being planned, and he gained much satisfaction from being involved with a building project for the latter years of the twentieth century, and beyond.

Just twelve months before retirement George suffered a stroke. He spent six months at home, but with his usual strength of purpose he returned to St. Mary's to complete the last sixth months of his professional career and to see his new school completed. "He saw it through!" said Mrs. Donkin.

Dorothy Whitehurst (nee Snow)

A pupil at Normacot Church of England Junior School in the mid 1930's, Dorothy won a scholarship to Thistley Hough Grammar School for Girls. She has clear memory of her years at Normacot and the many activities provided for the pupils.

"Like most of the girls, I dreaded the five minutes mental arithmetic tests at the end of morning and afternoon school. A series of 'quick-fire' numbers, delivered at speed by Mr. John Wylie, decided who went home a few minutes early and who stayed! The only time the morning assembly or our scholarship work was halted was when the telephone rang. It was kept on the headmaster's desk in the big room upstairs." The elevated dais of the early school had been retained and was still an excellent vantage point with its large desk and now its telephone. 'Silence' was required as soon as the telephone started to ring, everything stopped and the children seemed turned to stone!

"Inspite of arithmetic and English lessons every day we still had a full timetable of Scripture, History, Geography, Music, Nature Study, craft and sewing as well as physical training and games. The last hour on Friday afternoon was lovely because we chose books from the library cupboard; this was a change from reading round the class or chanting our tables while the register was marked! It was the only time when the big wall clock could be heard ticking, 'loudly.'

The third year class, taught by Mr. William (Bill) Wilkinson had the usual rows of desks, but round the perimeter were a number of cages containing grass snakes, newts, tortoises and beautiful green lizards. They were a wonderful source of interest for drawing, nature study and daily diaries charting the progress, or otherwise, of the, 'inmates!'

After the scholarship examination was over our school curriculum extended even further. I remember when Mr. Wylie gave a talk on heraldry, the divisions of the shield, family crests, the heraldic colours and their correct names. We were given a small template of a shield made of thin white cardboard and then we copied the crests of our Church and the City, so that we understood the broad concepts. Later, reference books were provided and we, 'tracked' the local aristocracy, their marriages with famous families and how their heraldic crests were put together.

The new, 'Free Art' using large brushes and easels was a joy. Reeves powder colours were easily mixed into any shade which you wanted; we had total freedom of design and some wonderful work was produced. Other activities for the summer included wood work, fret-work, weaving, sewing and embroidery, often to our own designs. All this activity culminated in the building of our own puppet theatre, making the hand puppets and their clothes and then presenting and performing our own, 'creation.'

Every year I looked forward to the annual Garden Fete held on the Vicarage lawn at the end of June. I was usually in the choir, dancing round the Maypole or enjoying country dancing under the, 'eagle-eye', of our teacher, Mrs. Ratcliffe. All the rehearsals for the boys physical training, the recorder band and the choir, made sure that the year ended on a, 'high' for both pupils and teachers.

Sentinel

Normacot School Choir at the Garden Fete 1937. Dorothy Snow is on the back row, 4th from the left. the author is on the third row far right

Back Row:
Eric Pool, ?, Sylvia Shenton, Dorothy Snow, Iris Bradburn, Dorothy Wright, Nora Tranter, ?, ?.

Third Row:
Joyce Wyatt, Harold Till, Kenneth Whithurst, Edna Colclough, Mary Webb, Margaret, Brenda Palmer, Derek Amison, Godon Birch, Mary Wilkinson.

Second Row :
Gilbert Jones, ?, Jean Toft, Olive Leese, Edna Barry, ?, ?, ?.

Front Row:
Kenneth Edwards, Gordon Ash, Ada Lawson, Sheila Walker, ?, Violet Bengry, Eric Newbon, Ronald Colclough

All this was achieved inspite of an old school building with no modern facilities, but what we did possess was a dedicated and caring headmaster and staff. The teachers knew every child by name and the names of their parents, so with this sense of belonging and good teaching, we gained in confidence. Many of us passed for the Grammar School and even those who did not had a wonderful start in life."

Music Teachers

Mrs May Taylor (nee Millington) 79, Upper Belgrave Road

May Taylor was my (the author) music teacher. She was a fine pianist and a member of a musical family. Her brother, Frank, was organist at Normacot Church for many years. May became the Stoke on Trent representative for the London College of Music and had total charge of both practical and theoretical examinations held at St. John's Church, Hanley. She was an excellent tutor and always made sure that Theory of Music kept pace with technical ability in voice or piano. Many of her pupils progressed from primary grade to Diploma and, also had a good musical knowledge to offer in School Certificate and if necessary, entry to Training College.

She always included stories about each composer of a 'set piece;' when and where he lived, details of his life and what other compositions he had written. From correct fingering and phrasing, she gradually introduced a concept of balance and form in each piece being studied. Key structures, or 'colours', were linked with theory and then related to the beauty and artistry in the music. May was a quiet, gentle and yet precise lady who obtained the best possible results from the many and very varied talents which found their way to her front door! I remember her with respect, affection and also with much gratitude for the excellent musical help which she gave to me in my formative years.

Miss 'Queenie' Hancock Chaplin Road

Derek Stoddard Remembers!

"The date of February 28th 1939 is engraved indelibly on my memory, for this was the day when aged ten, I had my first piano lesson from the redoubtable 'Queenie' Hancock. She was a lady of ineffable charm and glamour, who bore my faltering attempts to bang a tune out of her upright piano and to master the mysteries of minims, crotchets and semi-quavers with both patience and fortitude. I well remember her sitting beside me tapping a pencil in time to my playing with metronomic regularity, always looking elegant, beautifully 'made-up' she never flinched for a moment at my musical inadequacies. All this was for two shillings an hour!"

Thank you, Queenie, I still remember that, 'Every Good Boy Deserves Favour!' Incidentally, the very first piece of music I mastered was called, 'June Roses.' Later, I married a girl whose name was Rosemary June.

Alan Smith

Memories of Normacot C of E Junior School during the 1940's

"When the time came to go to the 'Big School' we were well into the war years. We still carried our gas masks and often practised 'shelter drill', but I can't recall the sirens sounding in the day-time though they did quite often at night; then we either slept in the Anderson shelter or in the pantry under the stairs until the, 'all-clear' wailed out. We never had a full scale air-raid, which was surprising in view of the proximity of the huge munitions factory at Swynnerton.

Activities connected with the war included the colouring in of a cyclostyled picture of an R.A.F., pilot sitting in a rubber dinghy in a choppy ocean, pre-sumable the North Sea, patiently awaiting the air-sea rescue launch. The prize for the best effort from the City schools was a National Savings Certificate, with National Savings stamps for the best entry from individual schools. Another imaginative competition required collecting waste paper. Depending on the amount collected, brightly coloured cardboard 'badges' were awarded, corresponding to different army ranks from 'private' to 'fieldmarshall' I fell short of the ultimate, but managed to make, 'general'.

Towards the end of the war we received food aid from Canada in the form of powdered chocolate; another way of obtaining 'extras' was when we lined the footpath in Meir Road as the American convoys rumbled by, cheering and yelling out, 'Got any gum, chum?' Very often we were fortunate in sharing out not only gum, but also chocolate bars. Strangely, on one occasion, we were handed turnips from a pile on the staff-room floor and told to chew on them steadily as they would do our teeth good! We used to 'Dig for Victory' in the large front garden of a house below the school, in Normacot Road, so perhaps these were the fruits of our labours and not the result of an over-enthusiastic local farmer's war-effort. Concern for our health included the regular visit of Nurse Bartlam, who weighed us, checked our height, teeth and finally our hair for the presence of the dreaded, 'nits'. Occasionally, sad to say, she found some.

As we were a church school, visits from Vicar Mountford, a mild and diminutive man, were quite frequent, particularly when preparing for days of note in the Church calendar. With Bible stories, parables and moral instruction, he did his best to set us on the path of righteousness.

Our curriculum stressed the three, 'R's' with preparation for the Scholarship being the centre of instruction during the last two years of schooling. However, from time to time we would enjoy a film show in the big downstairs room. Subjects varied from 'Steelmaking' or the 'Fishing Fleet' to an early, 'Mickey Mouse' or, 'Felix the Cat' cartoon, and then, in those days long before T.V., and video, joy would be unconfined! Our spirits were always high when the annual garden party, held on the lawn of the Old Vicarage required our presence and participation; the stalls, side-shows, bran tub, children's competitions of all types with sack races, potato races, egg and spoon and three legged races all contributed to the fun, as did the talent contests, camp-fire songs and sketches supplied by the Normacot scouts and cubs. The high-light of the Garden Party was the arrival of the Rose Queen with her retinue and her crowning by a distinguished visitor. This was followed by gymnastic displays, formal dancing and finally Maypole Dancing of a high and complicated order!

'Composed and elegant on the Great Day'

Circa 1943.

*'Carefree days
in a caring
community.'*

Circa 1945

The school buildings, ancient as they were, satisfied our educational needs; as with many schools of the period, one room led into another. The old exterior iron staircase leading to one of the upper storey classrooms was intended as a fire escape but even though a potential deathtrap, was used morning and afternoon as a means of entry and exit. No-one, to my knowledge, ever came to any harm by using it.

The school had an excellent reputation and children travelled quite a distance to take advantage of all it had to offer. Several came from different parts of the Meir, Meir Heath and Lightwood while most of us came from within half a mile of the school buildings. The headmaster was Mr. Eric Wilkinson, a respected member of a family who have been active in the teaching profession for several generations. Mrs Harvey taught the first class, while Mrs Ratcliffe, Mrs Gallagher, Mr. Cooke, Miss Lovatt and Mr. John Wylie, the deputy head-master, completed the teaching staff.

My progress was rapid and I really enjoyed school. It was a tightly knit unit and we acquired the basic social and academic skills at the hands of a dedicated teaching staff. However, I had two periods away from the classroom, firstly when playing with Michael Green in his father's builders yard at Eversley House. As I stood behind him, he hit me accidentally on the forehead with an iron bar. I was knocked out and the bruise assumed the shape of a hen's egg! Luckily, there were no permanent ill-effects. Shortly after this, the top class sat for the scholarship 'Intelligence Test' and the Maths and English sections of the '11 plus,' a misnomer as I was only nine and a half. Later, I sat for the entrance examination to Newcastle High School, to which I won a scholarship, when most entrants were fee-payers. Better still, I achieved first place for boys in the City '11 plus' examinations, with the oral examination waived. However, my parents decided that I would attend Longton High School in the September term.

The summer term was more relaxed with art and craft lessons, singing most of the songs in the, 'News Chronicle Song Book' and best of all, Friday afternoons when Miss Lovatt selected library books for us to read, according to our ability.

My last day at Normacot was spectacular! We were in the school yard playing a 'jousting' game involving some of us riding of the others' backs and generally charging around in a sort of hand to hand combat. A pair of 'combatants' cannoned into us unseen, from behind. We went down, I hit the floor, there was a sharp crack and an agonising pain hit my left leg below the knee; I had broken my leg! Mr. Cooke carried me to the nearby Cottage Hospital because there was no transport. My mother was sent for and my leg was set and plastered without any form of anaesthetic. Thus ended my last day at Normacot School in 1944!

Inspite of all this, I can look back at those days with a feeling of real achievement and fondness; these really were some of the, 'happiest days of my life.'

Betty Wardle (nee Eaton)

"Our life revolved around the school, church and Vicarage, or 'Haunted House' as the children called it. I was really happy at school, and although the teachers were strict, we were kept so busy that the cane was not used very often. However, one day I did get the cane and I must admit it was my own fault and I deserved it. One morning, I 'bobbed' school until about eleven o'clock. I had been in a friends house talking and my cousin, Jean Lowe, came and fetched me because normally I never missed a day at school. Mrs Harvey was our teacher and she told us to sit down on the front row and begin our work. My inkwell was empty and I took the other one on the desk. Jean said, "That's my inkwell!" and snatched it back. I held on and then let go, the ink flew out and landed on Mrs. Harvey. I was sent to the Headmaster and had two strokes of the cane; one for 'bobbing' and one for the ink! That was the only blot on my copy book, because I enjoyed everything else and had lots of friends. I remember being sad during a special assembly because one of our boys, Graham

Gerrard, had been killed while delivering papers on his bicycle, near Longton library. As we were a church school, we said prayers for him during every assembly that week.

Playtimes were lovely when we were allowed to go to Mr. Maish's shop just above the school; it's a hairdressers now. A large bottle of sodapop was only one old penny and you could get a bag of sweets mixed to your own choice for a halfpenny. Toffee whirls shaped like Catherine Wheels, mint imperials, liquorice all-sorts, 'gobstoppers' with a different colour for each layer and of course jelly babies. These and many more made our final choices difficult, but Mr. Maish was patience itself, even when we kept changing our minds. He knew we would visit again!

There were no computers or videos in school, so when we had some-one to give us a talk from the 'outside', there was great excitement. One day, a man who was deaf and dumb visited and with the help of a friend, showed us how he coped with life, by demonstrating some basic sign language. It was the first time that I had really thought about disability, and even now, when I watch the T.V., news being, 'signed' I remember his talk, all those years ago. To me, school was like belonging to one happy family; Mr. Eric Wilkinson was strict but kind and caring to us all. I miss those days a lot and it seemed strange that on my wedding day at Normacot Church, my old school was just opposite, waiting to be demolished.

A new life for Betty Eaton;
the end of an era for her old school
where the demolition notice is already in place.

Lorraine Salt (nee Jefford)

Normacot in the 1950's

Monday was wash day with the old boiler, mangle and dolly peg. As it was an all day job, the main meal was usually bread with 'dripping' from the Sunday joint. This was very early in the 1950's as my mother died in 1952. Our house in Buccleuch Road had no bathroom or inside toilet so we had to use the toilet at the top of the yard and a tin bath in front of the fire on, 'bath nights'. The toilets were box shaped and had wooden seats. I remember that Mrs Harris over the road had a double seat which her niece and I painted one day; Mrs Harris got paint on her best silk knickers and we stayed quiet for a few days!

In 1951, when I was five, Buccleuch Road had just been re-gritted and of course, I fell down and grazed my elbow. As my Mum was, 'heavy handed', I wouldn't let her touch it and so I waited until my Dad came home from work. By this time it had healed over, but when I was eleven, a small lump appeared and I had it removed at Longton Cottage Hospital. They found a small white stone which I kept for years on a piece of plaster and showed it proudly to anyone who would look.

Longton library was my greatest pleasure and from an early age I would take out six books at a time and escape into an enchanted land full of adventures. In those days we played hopscotch and because there was no fear of traffic interrupting our game, we drew the boxes on the road.
It was always exciting when the rag and bone man came with his horse and cart. You could hear him shouting two or three streets away, so you had plenty of time to find enough rags and bits and pieces to qualify for a balloon or a goldfish when he stopped by your door.

There were three small shops in Buccleuch Road, Fone's shop was half way up on the left, with Mrs Evan's shop opposite and Mrs West's shop was on the right near to the junction with Belgrave Road. These three shops served about ninety houses. My Dad had an account at West's with everything written down in a book so that every Friday, when he was paid, the bill was settled promptly.

Everywhere you turned in Normacot, there were shops which met all our needs. There was a chip shop just below the, 'Alhambra' and also one on the opposite corner. Chips were wrapped up in newspaper and they tasted and smelled good. You nearly always had large portions so that you would come again!

Further down there was the Co-op, a Post Office and then Barnish's fruit and vegetable shop facing down Chaplin Road.

Normacot Post Office circa 1955   Note the ink barometer by the door and the complete lack of litter in the street.

Number 34 Chaplin Road, was a grocer's shop and it still stands on the corner of Furnace Road. When I returned to Normacot in 1970, I ran this shop for four years. Tam's was another grocers opposite while further down Chaplin Road was Leese's butchers and just below, on the corner of short Hamilton Road was Hurst's bakery and shop. All their bread and cakes were made on the premises and the lovely smell of baking wafted for quite a way on six days a week. You just had to buy!

When the Reverend Williams was the Vicar, I went to Sunday School quite regularly and joined the Brownie Troupe which met in the Church Hall; we were very busy in the troupe and I enjoyed every minute of it. I'm sorry to say, that I wasn't always good. A retired teacher lived in the big house on the left hand corner of Upper Belgrave Road and we often used her garage door as a wicket; this did not go down well! At other times, if we were skating, we would hang onto the back of the coal lorry as it was driven down the street. This must have been in the late 1950's, because at the beginning of the decade coal and milk were still delivered by horse and cart. If it was dark, we played under the gas lamps nearby. Each street had a, 'backs' with two entries leading into the next street. Some entries had gates and if they were not locked, we would run down, shouting loudly and rattling tin cans. Of course, people came out of the houses to catch us, but we'd made good our escape by then.

My Dad worked on the kilns at Shaw and Copestake's and I often went to meet him so that we could walk home together along Normacot Road. I remember that the sky was always heavy with black smoke from the bottle neck kilns and when you hung any washing out, it was soon covered in black specks.

Photograph given by Mrs. L. Taylor

'On the Way to the Alhambra?'
Outside Ray Griffin's shop circa 1959.
Marie and Patricia Taylor

The Author

Houses reduced to rubble, streets disappearing, two departments of the
Co-op closed due to the construction of the A50.
Lilian Taylor is visibly upset by the 'new' Normacot.

Hollinson's Corner

Swept away by the new A50, Hollinson's Corner, which was the old Normacot boundary, no longer exists.

Standing at the junction of Meir and Uttoxeter Roads, it was a focal point for travellers from Longton to the Meir and also for those visiting Normacot, Blurton and Trentham. It was here that trams from the Pottery Towns turned, with much, 'clanking', ready for the long haul back to Stoke and beyond.

When Ewart and Gertrude Hollinson bought the shop, circa 1930, the Council advised them that extensive road-improvements were, 'on the books.' However, such is the speed of progress that on retirement they had escaped, with many years to spare, the trauma experienced by so many business people along the A50 route during the 1990's.

His daughter, Jean Gunn (nee Hollinson) took photographs of the shop in 1986. Her early life and that of her sister, Tess, was bound up in the property. "I had to have some record of our shop, it was such a wrench when everything was gone."

Photograph given by Mrs. Jean Gunn

*Hollinson's Shop and Snack Bar in
Uttoxeter Road 1986.*

"My Father started the business as a small general store selling sweets, tobacco, cigarettes and groceries. Fruit and vegetables were displayed outside, but even in those days, some items, 'disappeared' after small boys had passed by on the way to school!

Father was full of ideas for increasing trade. In 1943, he bought a house in Uttoxeter Road, 175, later 551, after the numbers were changed. It belonged to three sisters named Sutton. Two were well-known teachers and one, a successful dressmaker. With the extra space at the shop and the kitchen being renovated, he began to make and sell his own sausages and brawn. After a while, a new venture was on the agenda, 'Hollinson's Ice Cream!' It was a success from the start and was always known by the family name.

Soon he bought a number of bicycles and fitted them with small fridges which were secured to the front of the handlebars. He employed some boys to bring his, 'Outdoor Sales Department' into reality. They went to Longton Park and nearby streets trying their best to outdo the, 'Stop me and Buy One' trade of Wall's Ices! Of course there were accidents when bicycles tipped over or collided with something, but the boys seemed happy and we never noticed if they ate any of the profits during hot weather.

My Father's ideas reached a climax when he leased the upper floor as a hairdressing salon and opened the ground floor bay windowed room as a, 'Snack Bar!' It was popular with all the local people, but particularly so with commercial travellers who found it a convenient stopping place.

They parked their cars easily and safely in Meir Road and then had the choice of a short break with a sandwich and a pot of tea, or a more substantial lunch menu. A regular clientel developed and visited for many years.

'Hollinson's Corner' The A50, to Longton and Uttoxeter, is on the right and Meir Road is to the left of the picture.

Photograph given by Mrs. Jean Gunn

When Father was 67, Mother delivered her ultimatum, 'Retire!' They had achieved so much together and always provided us with a happy family life. Now, except for these photographs, I often feel it never happened.

Many people must feel regret when memories and places
are swallowed up by what is termed, 'progress'.

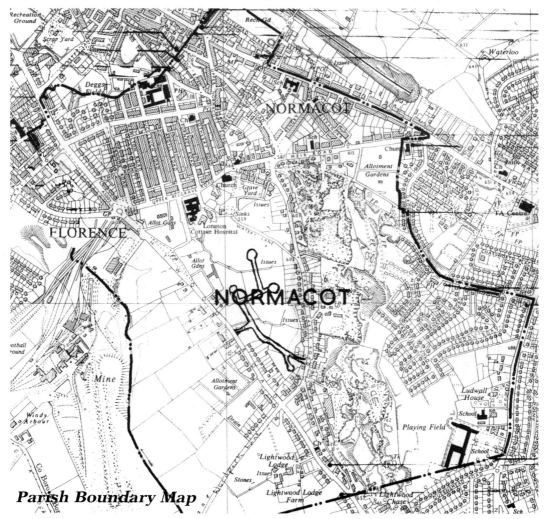

Parish Boundary Map

The 'proposed' development plan (circa 1960) has been joined (1998) by extensive building on the old Florence Colliery site. Local people and some councillors had hoped that indoor and outdoor leisure facilities would have been provided for the southern part of the City. Many parents wanted a modern school in a parkland setting to be part of the plan in what is a heavily populated area served by excellent schools in mostly outdated buildings.

This new housing estate has been achieved by Stoke-on-Trent Regeneration Ltd., and St. Modwen PLC.

ESSENTIAL SERVICES

Bengry's, The Normacot Bakers.

Over 100 years of service

Charles Bengry established his grocer's shop at the corner of Spring Road and Victoria Road (now Bengry Road) in 1890. From the beginning, it was a success. Charles was a far seeing businessman, so he apprenticed his son, Cecil, to Woods, the bakers, at the junction of Meir and Uttoxeter Roads.

When Cecil was sixteen years of age in 1893, and with his apprentice-ship completed, Charles set him up in business. This was in a small bakery at the bottom of the grocer's shop yard, in Spring Road.

Robert Bengry, the fourth generation of the family said, "In the early days, Cecil mixed the dough in a trough by hand, weighing and moulding was also done by hand. The brick built oven, part of the bakery structure was lined with fire-brick and needed constant care to maintain the correct temperature. Often, a special mop with long ribbon-like attachments had to be dipped into water and then flailed over the bottom of the oven. This 'mellowed' the heat and the resulting steam evened it out".

This second business flourished and soon Bengry's horse drawn van was delivering loaves, cobs and cakes to their customers in Normacot and to the villages of Barlaston and Fulford.

At this time, the stables were housed on the site of the present bakery. There was quite a deep well in front of them which had steps of the, 'Stairwell' type, descending at least a metre. This constant source of pure water was essential to the houses in the old Victoria Road, now Bengry Road, and was used regularly in Longton itself enabling carters and carriers to do good business.

Before the bakery was even envisaged, the presence of water helped a number of businesses to thrive on this site. A pickle factory traded for a time, as did a mineral water company, known as, 'Normacot Springs'. This was registered in the name of E. Tams described as an 'Aerated Water Manufacturer' in the 1881 Census. "We have found many bottles during alterations", said Robert Bengry. "They are of thick light green glass; each has a crimped neck and were supplied by Pilkington's of St. Helens".

*Looking to the Future?'
Cecil Bengry with his first motorised van.*

Cecil Bengry died in 1939, aged fifty-nine. Shortly after his death the bakery became a limited company owned by his four children.

When his son Harold Bengry, returned from his army service after the Second World War, he made many changes. Firstly, he became sole proprietor of the bakery. Then, in spite of the post-war building restrictions and shortage of materials, a new, mechanised bakery was built on the present site in Spring Road.

Now, there were two oil-fired ovens, two bakers, two drivers with four other men for van and bakery duties. With this staff, Harold was able to concentrate on the new administration and also his future planning of the bakery. The same outlets were maintained, but were expanded, due to the closure of smaller bakeries. These included Woods, where his father, Cecil, had served his apprentice-ship.

By 1976, all processes used electricity and the bakery had doubled in size. Gradually, many small, local shops closed, and Bengry's found that they were supplying the wholesale trade, in an ever expanding market.

Extensions were made again in 1995 and 1996. Robert Bengry said, "We have six vans now and 90% of our trade is wholesale. We supply hotels, public houses, caterers and takeaways. Our ovens are at least double the size of Harold's, and we're having to work round the clock to fulfil our orders. The bakery is still moving forward. Recently, we have had enquiries from Manchester to supply motorway service stations and wine bars. Already, the bakery is one hundred and five years old (1998) and is still expanding. We've always used quality ingredients and maintained the high standards and personal service of Cecil Bengry. This is the reason we are still in business, in a highly competitive trade".

However, the Bengry family has earned the respect and trust of local people in other ways.

Cecil Arthur Bengry (1880 -1938) was the Independent Councillor for Ward 26. He served on the finance, public assistance and library committees. His work for the Alexandra Road Methodist Church as both trustee and treasurer was outstanding; as was his work for the aged of the parish.

His son, Harold Ernest Bengry (1910-1994) was elected to the City Council for the same seat and served for six years. He was a dedicated Methodist becoming treasurer, trustee, Sunday School Superintendent of Christ Church, Meir Road as well as being a Circuit Steward. His interests extended to Longton Cottage Hospital, where again, he was a trustee and to Stallington Hospital, as a member of the Opening Committee.

Today, the business is in the capable hands of the fifth generation of the Bengry family. Malcolm, Robert's son, is in sole charge and the Company Secretary is Carolyn, Robert's daughter. 'Bengry's the Bakers', with its close family ties and its loyal workforce, is set fair for further success in the 21st Century.

The slogan on their vans in 1946 read,
'You Need it, we Knead it!'. How very true!

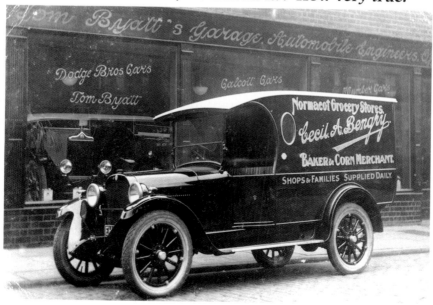

Photograph given by Mr. R. Bengry

Two well-known names - Byatt and Bengry

Photograph given by Mr. R. Bengry

The Bakery Today.
Letters of gold look down on part of the modern fleet,
which delivers over a wide area

Miss Vera Farmer

The daughter of S. R. Farmer, chemist and niece of Florence A. Farmer, Lord Mayor of Stoke -on-Trent (1931-32) Vera, now retired, has clear memories of her years in Normacot.

"Our pharmacy in Uttoxeter Road opened in 1907 and was well placed to serve the people of Normacot. It was in a row of small shops, facing what is now the Alhambra Roundabout. Dr. Carrington's surgery was directly opposite, while Dr. Richmond's, later Dr. Heslin's surgery was at the top of Chaplin Road.

Prior to 1947, doctors had both private and panel patients and throughout those years the local people came to us for medicine, or advice from my father. There were many poor families who could not afford a doctor's visit or even the prescribed medicine. In these cases, father would often advise on home-made remedies, or he would make up a bottle suitable for both patient or pocket. Others went to see Mrs Floyd, a lady who had some experience in health matters, assisting at births, identifying infections and who was also available for, 'laying out' when a death had occurred.

Miss Farmer with a well stocked shop circa 1970.
Note the gleaming mahogany and small drawers
for medicines under the rear shelving.

In the 1920's, well before the arrival of antibiotics and penicillin, some of the established remedies included Fenning's Lung Healers, which were tiny rough balls, difficult to swallow in spite of their size. Liquafrutta helped to soothe coughs, while Parrish's Chemical Food enriched the blood. In the Springtime, there was always a rush to buy Sulphur Tablets; these cured a, 'spotty' complexion which was the result of eating stodgy food during the winter; if this did not succeed, the next step was the dreaded Senna Pods, infused in hot water. They never failed! Cases of infection were always difficult to deal with, even if the doctor had visited. Father always advised that isolating the patient was of the utmost importance. Families in small, overcrowded houses resorted to hanging sheets soaked in Lysol over the bedroom door; this was often effective if there was a bowl of water in the room so that hands could be washed on entering or leaving. Tuberculosis, scarlet fever and meningitis were killers in those days, mainly because of inadequate hygiene and poor nutrition; often mothers had to cope in dreadful conditions.

The pharmacy was sold in 1976 and continued to trade as a chemist for a few years. Father and I were proud of the service we gave to the people of Normacot and also for the type of shop we retained in the face of, 'progress'. No refitting or refurbishment was even considered because we wished to retain the original Edwardian appearance of the shop. All the wood was mahogany; the fittings, show-cases and the individual drawers for medicines. The crafts-manship was superb and over the years the wood became even richer in col-our; it seemed to have the ability to, 'glow' at anytime of day or evening. One special feature of our pharmacy was the wrought iron spiral staircase; it was unique and I am so glad that it went to people who would appreciate it before the sale of the business was completed.

'The Last Day'
The end of an era. 1976

I was quite distressed, as were some local residents, when soon after the sale, the Edwardian interior was replaced by new fittings in the modern style of white wood, plastic and glass. The shop lost all its character. It was a privilege to know the people of Normacot and their families during so many years. War-time and peace-time saw many changes locally, but in 1947, the new Na-tional Health Service was the, 'saviour',when the very real fear of being ill and unable to obtain good care for your family, was removed, as we thought, for ever."

Picture given by Mrs. K. Brassington

'At the Blacksmiths'

Arthur Barnish (at the back of the picture) with Dolly the second, and faithful Bess.

The forge, at the top of Engine Bank, was opposite to the present day Gladstone Pottery Museum.

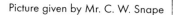

Picture given by Mr. C. W. Snape

Arthur Thomas Barnish

Grocer and Coal Merchant - 81 Upper Normacot Road

Originally, Barnish's shop belonged to Mrs. Bloor, the mother of Mrs. Annie Barnish. It had always sold fruit and vegetables from the turn of the century and to this day it has changed very little.

Mrs. Barnish was in charge of the shop while her husband, Arthur, delivered coal and vegetables to most of Normacot. Every day and evening, except Sunday, Arthur, his loaded cart and Bess, his black labrador, could be seen working until quite late at night. At dusk, a small lantern was hung on the back of the cart as they continued their steady, unhurried way around the streets of Normacot.

During his working life Arthur had two horses called 'Dolly.' The first one was black and about eighteen hands high. She was quiet, fond of apples, and the children loved her, often following the cart in the hope of a ride.

Ready for the long day ahead
Dolly circa 1935

Picture given by Mrs. K. Brassington

When Dolly was crippled by a nail in her hoof, Arthur borrowed a black and white, 'pinto' to pull the cart. However, she had one fault; she hated to be alone and one morning when pastured in Star and Garter Road, she jumped the gate, walked into Meir Road, made her way along Upper Normacot Road and arrived at the back gate just as the family was starting breakfast!

His second, horse, 'Dolly' was smaller, but helped Arthur to play his part in the 1953 Coronation Celebrations. Kath Brassington, his grand-daughter said, "Arthur's cart was decorated with paper ribbons of red, white and blue. I dressed as Britannia and my friends were characters from history. We visited all the street parties from the top of Chaplin Road to Lightwood Road. Arthur, with Dolly and Bess, was cheered by everyone. We were in Belgrave Road when it started to rain and in minutes the ribbons and costumes were ruined. No-one wanted to give up because we had a new Queen and it was our Coronation Day too!"

"After a while some of the small children left our procession and went home, but all over Normacot the parties and rejoicing went on for hours. In those days there was very little T.V., and people just talked and laughed together. When the rain cleared, nearly everyone came outside and danced the conga along the street and up every entry. Next day there were quite a few headaches and lots of sore throats!"

Barnish's shop was always busy; Lymer's buses ran tours from there. The trip on Thursdays was to Sandbach Market. On Sunday, there was an, 'Evening Circular' which started at 6.30 p.m., returning at 10.30 p.m., after visiting outlying villages in the beautiful and easily accessible countryside which still exists today. Marchington was a favourite place to stop for a drink and sandwiches. Inevitably, the return journey included an enthusiastic 'sing-song!' For Bank holidays and the local 'Potters' break, Rhyl and Blackpool were popular venues and were always heavily booked; both of these holiday resorts gave good value for money and excellent entertainment for children and adults.

During the 1950's there was a vogue for Marching Bands, some of which have survived to the present day. Mr. Arthur Barnish, (Junior) and his wife, Emily, organised the Normacot, 'Tartan Drummers' who entertained at Longton Park for important events and competed against troupes from other parts of the Potteries, and beyond. They were about twenty-five in number, all well-rehearsed and outstandingly smart in their tartan regalia.

The Tartan Drummers circa 1960 Extreme right - Kath Brassington (Arthur's grand-daughter)

Picture given by Mrs. K. Brassington

Barnish's shop is now owned by Eva Brain (nee Dawson) and outwardly there has been little change. Inside, however, Eva has extended the range of fruit, vegetables, cakes and sweets, to keep pace with the changing needs of Normacot. It is one of the few non-Asian shops still trading in the area. During the days of the 1930's Depression and the ration book era of the war years, visiting this shop was the, 'high spot' of the week for the children who came to buy their 'treats'. Today, in these more affluent times, the colourfully dressed Asian children often visit daily but their excitement and anticipation can never measure that felt by children of a bygone era of clogs, and 'hand-me-down' clothes who so often felt a real fear of both the present and the future.

MR F. W. WELLS

69, Upper Normacot Road
For All Cycle Requirements' Parish Magazine Advertisement 1953

Mr. 'Tufty' Wells, known as such, because of the magnificence of his luxuriant, if droopy moustache, had a bicycle shop in Upper Normacot Road, directly opposite Chaplin House. He always dressed in brown overalls and was rarely seen without an oily rag in his hands.

His shop was a converted terrace house. The one or two new bicycles on show in the window, made the shop seem much darker and smaller that it really was. Repaired bicycles were propped round the walls, as were the near, 'wrecks,' left by their hopeful owners. Everyone knew that if Mr. Wells could not make a bicycle roadworthy, then no-one would succeed. All this hope, trust and endeavour was generally taking place while mysterious, but not unpleasant kitchen aromas, mingled with the oily smells of the repair shop.

Time did not seem to be of great importance in the relatively relaxed days of the 1930's and 'Tufty' always made me, as a child, feel welcome and confident whenever I made the journey to his shop. Sometimes, it was to have a wireless battery recharged; on other occasions, he inspected my red and gold fairy cycle for chain trouble and bell inadequacy. This was with the dedicated expertise one associates with a modern day, 'pit-stop,' but not with the same speed!

A solitary petrol pump graced the, 'forecourt' of his shop. It had a bar which swung outwards, a gauge and a winder. There was much competition for the honour of 'winding' amongst the children, as there were few cars and lorries in Normacot and when one vehicle stopped for petrol, great excitement ensued.

Mr. Wells did not live in Normacot; he came from Congleton, where he was a bell-ringer of some repute. For a number of years, he travelled daily in a car which had hardly any floor and the driver's seat lacked springs.

'Tufty' overcame this latter defect by placing an accumulator battery underneath the seat for support. The horn could be temperamental and would not stop sounding unless drastic measures were taken. A few blows with a large spanner usually sufficed! Needless to say, this mode of transport gave concern to both police and populace. So much so that complaints were made and his car was, 'confiscated,' by the police, during the Second World War.

Today, in a Normacot which has changed in so many ways, his shop is still there, albeit selling Asian food and not bicycles. Many people still remember him for his patience, kindness and the, 'honest job' he always achieved for his customers. Mr. Wells is buried in Congleton Churchyard and if there is a, 'hereafter,' I hope he is driving the car of his dreams and that the large spanner of yesteryear, is no longer necessary.

Leonard Shirley Leese, Master Butcher (1889 - 1969)

Mr. Leese came from Stone, where his family were farmers' butchers. His shop was on the corner of Buccleuch Road and from the early days circa 1912, was a great success.

His daughter, Marie said, "He was always busy and go ahead. Father sold home-made pork pies to the public houses in the area, but he wanted to be different from the other suppliers. He made a visit to Hunt's in Sheffield and bought a hand operated pork-pie maker. This consisted of a dozen tins on a block, with a handle to pull down. This crimped and stamped the pies, which were square in shape. He advertised and sold them as, 'Square Meals'. These were sold as far afield as Hanley, Bagnall and Goldenhill."

Later, he installed what can only be described as an 'Early Freezer Department'. He had a trap door cut into the floor of the shop, directly above the cellar, into which was put a large, insulated lead box. This had a gap between the outer walls to hold the ice. "The trap door was very secure," said Marie, "Father joked that he wanted no references made to Sweeney Todd!" The ice was brought, from, Waddell's of Shelton, in blocks measuring 4' by 2'. They were too big for the trap door and were broken up on the pavement outside the shop. There was a drain box leading to an outside grid which took the ice-water away.

Mission completed;
ice-picks at the ready!

Picture given by Mrs. Marie Walter

All the ice was transported in one or two of Leonard's lorries. He also had a transport business trading as, 'Leese & Corbet'. The coming of electricity had made his 'Freezer Department' possible and Market traders from Longton were often seen arriving with their vans and carts when they needed storage for surplus goods. "Meat in the ice-box, Len?" was their worried cry, as they reached the corner shop.

Leonard Leese was tall, dark and handsome. He possessed a fine, light baritone voice, and was much in demand at Police Concerts. He had a choice of professional accompanists; Arthur Coleman from the 'Alhambra' cinema, in Normacot and Camille ('Cammy') Bogart from the Empire Theatre in Commerce Street, Longton.

His daughter, Marie said "There were always, great preparations when a concert loomed! His dress suit and shirt were laid out on the bed. His gold cuff-links were placed ready on the dressing table while his shoes and gold Albert watch and sovereign were polished, usually by me!" His singing of 'Macushla' and Gilbert and Sullivan arias were popular at Police Concerts. However, they were often heard in the shop too. Harassed housewives had to wait for the, 'finale' while Leonard held one hand over a large knife, which was embedded in the block, and gesticulated with the other, whilst his captive audience fumed!

Still Singing?

Picture given by Mrs. Marie Walter

Transport to and from his concerts was also in the grand manner; he was a member of the Vintage Car Club and possessed many cars of interest, including a Model 'T' Ford and a Coventry Premier.

Marie remembers Normacot with affection. "It always seemed to be summer. There was no traffic, only father's van. Often we took some chalk and drew a 'tennis court' in the road; and at half-time mother served us home-made lemonade through the sash window. Father was the agent for Greatbach's 'Premier' bottling works at the top of Chaplin Road so we often had bottled lemonade with a marble for the stopper or ginger beer in the big stone jars."

In 1926, all was not well with some of her friends. "The strike brought deprivation where only a little poverty had existed before. Mother started a daily soup kitchen. Scraps and bones from the shop were boiled up with vegetables and pearl barley, to make a meal of sorts". Loaves were given by the bakers, 'Hawley and Sherwin' at the corner of short Hamilton Road. "The only snag," said Marie, "There was never much meat left on father's bones!"

The shop continued to trade as a butcher's for nearly thirty years after Len's death in 1969. It served a mixed local community, but the 'dramatic' business transactions and the heartfelt renderings of, 'Macushla' were gone forever. The house is now a private dwelling.

JOHN DAWSON - UNDERTAKER (1856 - 1927)

The Dawson family served the people of Normacot for three generations. They knew the bereaved families personally, and so, with the highest of standards, were able to give much comfort in times of distress.

The first business was established by John Dawson, circa 1880. This was in Reservoir Road, near to the Recreation Ground in Normacot. In 1896 he moved to 90, Alexandra Road with his new partner, Roland Slater.

By all accounts, John was a large, handsome man, with a powerful build and a character to match. "He had a distinct presence," said his grandson, Jack. "Also, according to the family, his shirts were reputed to be three times whiter than anyone elses!"

John Dawson - Founder of the Firm.

John Dawson was Clerk and Sexton to Normacot Church for forty-five years. His son, Harry, was a regular soldier, serving in India, the Boer War and the 1914 -18 War, After being invalided out of the army, he joined his father in the family business, but he died of shrapnel wounds in 1928. He left two young

sons, Harry and Jack as well as two daughters Eva and Minnie. His 1901 diary of daily events in the Boer War, written in superb 'copper-plate', is a valuable history of hardship and discipline experienced on campaign by the British soldier. It is worthy of detailed study. His widow, Sarah Ann (Sally) a lady of indomitable spirit and strength of character, took over all the responsibilities of both family and firm, acting as Clerk and Sexton from 1927 until 1966.

Sally Dawson

The work was hard and so were the times. Sally made sure that when her sons were old enough, they served full apprenticeships as joiners, and were, therefore, skilled men. She trained them in all aspects of the work and expanded the business in every way. During the Second World War, Sally was in complete charge of matters until Harry returned home in 1946. As the son of a regular soldier, Harry remembers when he let family standards slip! Returning to his unit he reached Crewe station and realised that his only defence against the Germans was a large fruit cake which Sally had baked for him; his rifle was still at Normacot Station! After a quick phone call, the rifle was rescued by Jack and transported by headmaster Eric Wilkinson, thereby avoiding the disgrace of a court-martial. "Unlike my father, I didn't like army life and disliked the food even more"! said an unrepentant Harry.

Harry Dawson

Harry recalls that during Sally's ninetieth birthday celebrations with family and friends, she was plied with champagne and enjoyed the occasion immensely. However, she had to ask, "How much did that cost, Harry?" Sally was still in charge and therefore needed to know! Sally Dawson died in 1985 aged ninety-six, well respected in Normacot, where she spent all her life.

In 1954, the business moved to 105, Upper Normacot Road and prospered for many years. Later, in 1970, Jack moved to premises in Uttoxeter Road, while Harry remained at 105. Both brothers have spoken of the many changes they have seen during their working life.

Harry told me that, "It only cost sixpence to have the banns read in church; the church-yard grass was cut by hand, twice a year and in 1936, horses belonging to a Mr. Rowley , of Bengry Road, grazed near to the double gates of the church yard". Early in the church's history, these gates were used regularly by the horse drawn hearses, so as to gain access to certain parts of the grave yard!

"The greatest changes took place when our Asian clients came to see us," said Harry. "Some of their Religious customs were unknown to us. However, we met their needs and all was well."

Jack has a story which could be deemed an undertaker's 'nightmare.' An interment was taking place at Normacot and the verger noticed that there was a weakness in the ground. He whispered, "Don't let the Vicar get too close," but in vain. The cleric slid into the grave, albeit in a highly dignified manner, and whilst the mourners looked on in disbelief, Jack grabbed the Vicar's hand, and with help, hauled him out again, saying, "No Father, it's not your turn yet!" Jack declined to name the Vicar, who might, or might not have been aware of this quotation from Dr. Johnson (1709 - 1784)

"An odd thought strikes me, we shall receive no letters in the grave!"

Both brothers continued the high standards set by John Dawson, the founder of the business, and Sally, their mother. Meticulous in every respect, they have records which are a social history in themselves.

Jack has details of charges applying throughout his career;

1958 - Interments & Service	£ 6.00
- Interments, Service & Organ	£ 8.00
1970 - Interment, Service	£20.00
1983 - Interment, Service	£31.00
1996 - Interment, Service	£66.00

After 1970, no new graves were possible, in Normacot Churchyard.

Harry has completed a unique and detailed plan of the names and locations of every grave in Normacot Churchyard thereby retaining for posterity the names of local people respected in the pottery industry, politics, science, law and teaching. A keen Scout, Harry gave years of service, as Chairman of the Scouts Hall Committee, seeing them through many difficult times, as well as serving with distinction in the Scout Movement.

Jack Dawson

Although both brothers have retired, Jack in 1986 and Harry in 1995, the name, 'Dawson' remains in Normacot. New owners serve a changed and ever changing village, but the same high standards remain.

"Sally would not allow anything less," said Jack.

£ 6 : 0 : 0

Dormacot Church,

Dec 9th 1940

Received from Mrs Hallam

Sandon Road _____ (Ect parishioner)

the sum of _____ six _____ Pounds,

_____ Shillings, _____ Pence,

Fees for a Reserved Burial Space in Normacot Churchyard, including the cost of First Interment, that of the late

Mr Samuel Hallam

SPACE NO. a 2 8 1   H Dawson Clerk

W. E. Afford

Vicar

Document given by Mr. R. Hallam

John Edward Simmister Builder (1864-1946)

Simmister was a carpenter and his partner, Louis Clifford Green was a brick-layer; both were skilled men. Their partnership began just before Mr. Green married Miss Rose Simmister, a teacher, in 1923. Previously, the two men had owned a grocer's shop in Buccleuch Road, Normacot, and when sufficient funds had accumulated, they established their building business at 'Eversley House' in Upper Normacot Road.

The first workshop 1923. Note the neat work clothes, collars and ties. Mr. Green is wearing the trilby hat.

Picture given by Mr. R. Green

From the start, they decided that quality of materials and a high standard of workmanship would be their principal concerns. Mr. Reg. Green, grandson of Mr. Simmister said, "They had an excellent business, but were never as rich as they might have been. If it were a choice between money or quality, quality won. This is always the way with real craftsmen."

In those days, business depended on the recommendation of satisfied custom-ers. They were never short of work, even during the difficult years of the 1930's. Their houses can still be seen and are evidence of sound building practice. They built properties in the newer part of Chaplin Road, Short Ham-ilton Road and Windsor and Roxburgh Avenues. Lightwood Road, Ludwall Road and Sandon Road, Meir Heath, near to St. Francis Church show further examples of their excellent work.

Their only detached house in Normacot was 5 Windsor Avenue. This was where my brother Robert, and I grew up. According to Mr. Green's records for 30th November 1935, the costing of our house was as follows:

Purchase price	£625
Extras:	
Gate (1)	£ 6. 10. 0
Gate (2)	£ 3. 10. 0
Flagged path	£ 6. 18. 0
Garage	£ 20. 00. 0
Door Handles	£ 5. 16. 0
Lights	£ 1. 00. 0
Towel Rail	7. 6
<u>Total Cost</u>	<u>£ 669. 1. 6</u>

The Author

5 Windsor Avenue

This bought a spacious three bedroomed house, with a very large garden, enclosed by a six foot fence. All the windows and the front door had coloured decorative glass. The kitchen and hall floors were of 'terrazzo' for easy cleaning. High quality wood was used for the solid doors, picture rails and bannisters. There were two toilets and a modern bathroom.

Simmister & Green

During the 1930's over thirty men were employed on a regular basis, most of them from the closely knit community of Normacot. These included members of the Redman and Steele family as well as a skilled plumber, Jack Bradbury. Reg Green remembers him quite clearly, from childhood. "He always wore his trilby turned up all round, while his yellow overalls and bicycle clips seemed to be attached to him, permanently. What was of real interest to me, as a child, was that if he lost his temper, he never shouted, but ground his teeth audibly , for ages!"

Picture given by Mr. R. Green

Reg is the boy in the white shirt. Louis Clifford Green, is directly in front of him. John Edward Simmister - is sitting on the wheelbarrow, which he made during his apprenticeship training.
Note the lorry, which set Simmister apart from the handcarts used by the others!

Reg Green, now retired from teaching and his many years of distinguished service in the Scouting movement, recalled his early days with affection, and summed up by saying,

"They were happy, secure days in Normacot. Everyone knew each other and home, school, church and scouts, all seemed to merge. We had everything we needed."

BIBLIOGRAPHY

1. Staffordshire and Stoke-on-Trent Archives:
Log Books: Normacot National/C of E Junior Schools:
SAED 121 - 1863 - 1865
SAED 122 - 1885 - 1900
SAED 123 - 1880 - 1910
SAED 124 - 1940 - 1956

2. Log Books: Normacot C of E Infants School:
D3556/1/1 1877 - 1912
SAED 180 May 1961 - December 1978
SAED 181 January 1979 - August 1983
SAED 186 Items relating to school closure 1983

3. SAED 182 Admission Registers 1943 - 1977
SAED 183 Admission Registers 1978 - 1983
SAED 185 Correspondence re: proposed new school 1977

4. SP843-27 Normacot Parish Magazine September 1973
SP136-9 Scout and Guide Headquarters opening celebrations 1975

5. Report on School Board District of Longton 1871 - 1892

6. Wilkinson Family Papers:

i. Parish Magazines 1953 -1963 Rev. Beaver
ii. Parish Magazines January 1972 Rev. Beaver
September 1977 no incumbent
November 1979 no incumbent
iii. Data from the Etruscan Lodge Wm Wilkinson
iv. A Survey of Education 1920 - 1968 R. W. E. Wilkinson
v. "Before and After the Haddow Report" R. W. E. Wilkinson
vi. "The Impact of Plowden" R. W. E. Wilkinson
vii. National Union of Teachers Journals 1958 and 1961

Further Sources:

Normacot and it's Church Rev. C. Beaver
Blurton Chapel and It's Endowments Rev. S. W. Hutchinson 1912

"Years of Endeavour 1886 - 1907" G. Leveson-Gower
"A History of the Stoke-on-Trent and District Teachers' Assoc., 1878 - 1978" O'Rourke
"A Sociological History of Stoke-on-Trent" Warrilow 1960
"History of the Borough of Stoke-on-Trent" Ward 1843 (Reprint 1984)
"Clayhanger" Arnold Bennett, Penguin (997) 1954
"T. C. Wild, My Father" Nora Wild Hanley Reference Library
"Verses to Queen Victoria" T. C. Wild Hanley Reference Library
From Domesday Book to Magna Carter, Poole O. U. P., 1951
King John, Dr. W. L. Warren Methuen 1961

CONTRIBUTORS

I wish to acknowledge my indebtedness to those who have shared their childhood memories, family events and life in Normacot. After meeting and talking to so many people, it is obvious to all of us that,

"Our childhood never ends, it simply moves on".

M. Akram
S. Akram
G. Ash *
R. Bengry
Father S. Carter
R. Cooper
H. Dawson
J. Dawson *
K. Edwards
R. Green *
L. Goodwin

R. Hallam
B. Harrington
Monsignor J. Heslin
E. Leese *
K. Locker
S. Mitchell M. B. E.,
S. T. Mountford
Said Rasool Khalifa

Hafiz Dil-Kurshid
Father J. Pawson

Mansoor Rabani
F. Redman
Hafiz Siddiqui
S. Slater
A. Smith
C. W. Snape
L. Tranter
C. Turner
J. G. Wallis
T. Wilkinson
J. V. Wylie

Mr. Mrs E. Drew,
Mr. Mrs D. Gray,
Mr. Mrs G. Hurst,
Mr. Mrs G. Mills

Hazel Bagguley
Edna Barry
Carol Bennett
Kathleen Brassington
Kathleen E. Dean
Rhoda Donkin
Margaret Edge
Vera Farmer *
Jean Forster
Nancy Gosling
Jean Gunn
Carol Harratt
Nancy Henshall
Ada Hurst *
Jean Jones
Jean Livingstone
Nora Lovatt
Winifred Lovatt *
Gladys Parkes

Mary Perry
Catherine Radford
Sally Ralphs
Rosamund Rhodes
Charlotte Ridge *
Edna Ridge *
Barbara Rogers
Kathleen Rogers
Lorraine Salt
Angie Stevenson
Mary Sutton
Lilian Taylor
Jane Tunnicliffe
Marie Walter
Betty Wardle
Winifred Adams Webb
Mary Webb
Dorothy Whitehurst *
Audrey Williams
Emmy Williams

* Contributors who are now deceased

"No love, no friendship can cross the path of our destiny, without leaving some mark forever"
François Mauriac.